Ask yourself:
- What kind of relationship do I deserve?
- Am I consistently attracted to a certain psychological type?
- In that same sense, what "type" am I?
- Why do relationships that start off with such promise leave me in the ashes within a few months?
- Have there been major changes in who I am, and have my romantic relationships kept pace?
- Is it possible to find a love relationship that lasts forever?

CHOOSING LOVERS will help you answer these and many other questions about relationships and help you find the love that's right for you.

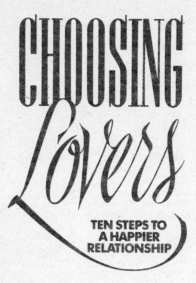

CHOOSING
Lovers

TEN STEPS TO A HAPPIER RELATIONSHIP

MARTIN BLINDER, M.D.
with Carmen Lynch, M.S.W.

AVON BOOKS  NEW YORK

"A Story Wet as Tears," by Marge Piercy from *Stone, Paper, Knife*. Copyright 1983, Alfred A. Knopf, a division of Random House. Printed with permission.

Portions of this book originally appeared in *Cosmopolitan* magazine.

All names have been changed, and events altered to protect confidentiality.

AVON BOOKS
A division of
The Hearst Corporation
105 Madison Avenue
New York, New York 10016

Copyright © 1989 by Martin Blinder, M.D.
Published by arrangement with Glenbridge Publishing Ltd.
Library of Congress Catalog Card Number: 88-83381
ISBN: 0-380-71201-6

First Avon Books Printing: February 1991

AVON TRADEMARK REG. U.S. PAT. OFF. AND IN OTHER COUNTRIES, MARCA REGISTRADA, HECHO EN U.S.A.

Printed in the U.S.A.

RA 10 9 8 7 6 5 4 3 2 1

*To my parents
and their forty-one-year love affair*

How quick bright things come to confusion.
Romeo and Juliet

All people can be seduced once but keeping them is
another matter.
New Chinese Proverb

Practice makes perfect.
The McGuffey Reader

Contents

Acknowledgments   xi

I. Introduction: The Romantic Relationship   1

II. Faces of Love:
The Shape of Romantic Relationships   5
  Validating Relationships—
    Covering the Holes   6
  Structure-Building Relationships—
    Constructing a Framework   16
  Experimental Relationships—
    Finding What Fits   24
  Avoidance Relationships—
    Playing It Safe   29
  Fusion Relationships—
    Trying to Stand   36
  Healing Relationships—
    Binding the Wounds   41
  Transitional Relationships—
    Moving Forward   46
  Synergistic Relationships—
    Having It All   51
  Summary   56

III. Components of Romance:
**How We Make Our Choices, Why Some Work
and Why Some Don't**   58
  Fit   58
  Need   66
  Sexuality, Monogamy and Trust   73
  Summary   77

IV. Your Love Relationships—And You 83
    The Time to Make Changes 85
    Evolution—Having It Different 87
    Revolution—Breaking the Pattern 90
    Summary 103

V. We've Been Having a Few Problems, Doctor 104
    Miscommunication 106
    Misperception 111
    Unmet Dependent Needs 116
    Threats to Adaptive Defenses 122
    Fear of the Unfamiliar 126
    Summary 131

VI. Effecting Repairs 133

VII. Why Love Ends 142
    Final Processes 143
    Love's End Lies in Its Beginnings 148
    Danger Signals 150

VIII. Remedies 152

Acknowledgments

Many of the ideas explored here evolved in collaboration with my long-time associate, inspiration, and friend, social worker Carmen Lynch, a truly original thinker and brilliant clinician. It is to Carmen that I owe the concept of relationship morphology and a seminal operative theme of this book: that even hugely unhappy, painful and seemingly destructive love relationships in fact constitute *adaptation* rather than *psychopathology*—psychological *evolution* rather than *disorder*; that each teaches us what we most need to know when we most need to know it; and that our serial choice of lovers is perhaps the most visible, objective measure of our emotional growth and development.

For the stimulus to gather my inchoate thoughts and scattered clinical experience into a book, I am indebted to Teresa Chris and Renée Golden, both of whom may be counted upon to cheerfully go well beyond the call of commercial duty, somehow devoting already crowded days to nurturing yet another new writer and his literary offspring.

For uncommonly literate word processing that miraculously transforms my chicken scratches and dictated mumbles into at least comprehensible—if not always graceful—prose, I have long been and remain utterly dependent upon Mary Lou Coyle, Goolcher Wadia and Janey Young.

Finally, as well as first, I thank my patients of twenty years who have entrusted their psyches for healing to my not always certain hand.

Martin Blinder, M.D.
San Anselmo, California

I

Introduction:
The Romantic Relationship

We are tangling, you and I, with an exhilarating but perilous subject. When romantic love strikes the heart, even the most profound and self-assured of thinkers are left dumbfounded and uneasy: Although the impetus for enduring symphonies and sonnets, it was romantic love that reduced the Prince of Wales to de facto commoner, and leveled Troy.

Romantic love precipitates disconcerting career changes. The engineer turns poet, the schoolmarm a femme fatale, the clerk a hunter, the philosopher an adventurer, the artisan an artist. Pragmatics obsess with far-fetched schemes, the wary turn reckless, the eloquent fall silent, the mute sing.

Yet, seemingly heedless of consequence, so swiftly do most of us initiate this cataclysmic state that, as recently calculated by a scholarly French statistician, somebody leaps into love every seven and two-thirds seconds. Although such peculiarly Gallic precision is suspect, it is nonetheless startling just how little we really know about a process that captures so many, so often, so easily, and to such irrevocable effect. Rarely have we enough data to fathom why in heaven's name our friends pick the mates they do. And usually, we're

1

too close to our own no less perplexing romantic experiences to see them with any greater clarity.

The astonishing number of books and articles addressing romantic love is a measure of both our fascination and our frustration with this elusive subject. Most of them ultimately fail to satisfy, I think, because they mistake a part of the process for the whole, like the three fabled blind men who, respectively feeling the trunk, tail, and back of the elephant, came up with vastly different ideas regarding the kind of animal before them. Or they may be unduly personal, focusing too narrowly on one individual's experience to enlighten the rest of us.

My goal for this book, then, is for you and I to stand back a bit and try to look at "romance" in its *entirety*. We shall explore how we fall in love and select our partners, the varied configurations our love may take and what we might expect from each, how things can seem to go terrifically well and then not so well, how love brings both fulfillment and discontent, the kinds of misjudgments our romantic feelings commonly compel (and how not to make them), how we fall out of love, and, finally, how best to enable love to last forever.

Doubtless my relentlessly systematic, unsentimental approach to these tantalizing conundrums is not without its own defects. But it has the virtue of bearing the fruits of psychotherapeutic work with many hundreds of couples in various stages of love, who over two decades have persistently raised, and will help us answer, such urgent, yet timeless questions as:

Why, of all the people in the world, did I fall in love with him (her)?

Why do I keep falling in love with people like *that*?

Are my love affairs random experiences, or do they fall into a pattern?

What sort of patterns of romance are there, and how can I recognize them?

Do I send out some signal that attracts one kind of lover and puts off others?

Do people love in the same way each time?

Can love be changed?

Is there such a thing as "neurotic love"? How is it different from "healthy love"? What kind of lover am I?

Why does love make some people happy and me miserable? Why does it last for a few people, but not for most?

What are the warning signs of love in danger?

Is there some discernible secret to everlasting love?

Why do some people have all the luck?

What inspires so much uncertainty and, indeed, what makes all love relationships, from adolescent crushes to lifelong marriage, so intriguing and complex, is that they involve (at least) two people in constant motion and flux. Should they share certain fundamental psychological processes, they may evolve and develop often with little introspection, along much the same clear path and so stay together as they grow older. We all know of couples who fall in love at age seventeen and remain connected for perhaps half a century.

But most couples, even those fortunate in their ability to form a broadly congruent intimate connection, are unlikely to *continue* to evolve together in all the myriad ways that go to make up a romantic bond. One partner or the other is likely to angle off, or move a little faster or a little slower, or simply stop. So the majority of us enjoy (or suffer) a number of somewhat shrouded interactions of varying lengths we call "love" throughout the course of our lives.

That we fall in love with a particular person at a particular time may not be quite preordained, but, as we shall see, our personality structure and degree of emotional maturity make our choice of partner remarkably predictable. We do not fall in love by coincidence. Who we select as lovers, how we relate to them, and the reasons we ultimately leave them (or they us) follow an inexorable psychological logic.

In the pages that follow, let us pursue that logic step-by-step, observe its influence on the lives and loves of others, and, as we do so, discern something of its impact upon our own. Let us explore the varied forms of romantic love—the patterns within the passion, the powerful forces that draw men and women to seek intimacy from each other, and the many different things people mean when they say, "I love you." You will be able here to sit in on psychotherapy sessions where we shall look at why people choose the lovers they do, why one couple's intimate relationship is so different from that of another, why love often brings conflict and pain, and finally, why romance endures for some and not for others.

In short, let us freeze for a few moments a moving, swirling image—and glimpse the reality within the magic.

II

Faces of Love:
The Shape of
Romantic Relationships

At first blush there may seem as many kinds of romantic love as there are lovers. But as we study the hidden, subconscious forces and desires bringing two people together and holding them there, eight separate and discreet patterns—eight ways of making intimate connections—repeatedly emerge. Although the course of maturation leads most of us through several types of romantic relationships during our lifetimes, there is surprisingly little immediate overlap of these distinctive patterns, and change from one to another comes very slowly. We all tend to be stubbornly loyal to our subconscious needs, sometimes at great cost.

You probably won't have much difficulty fitting yourself (or most of yourself) and your "significant others"—past or present—into at least one of the more orthodox of these patterns. Such discernment should provide a clearer sense of your relationships with those who are or have been important in your romantic life, of why you make the choices you do, and of what the future is likely to bring. The best way of figuring out and influencing where love is *going* is to understand where it's *been*. A better informed choice now may make unnecessary your having to choose a lover ever again.

Validating Relationships—Covering the Holes

"Richard is boring. Stupid and boring. Now *you're* interesting, doctor. *He's* stupid and boring."

I believed my patient, Diana, to be sincere but doubted the objectivity of her comparison. So I asked, "Richard invents this little device in a single evening at the age of twenty-nine, gets it accepted by computer schools across the country by age thirty, is a multi-millionaire at age thirty-one, and you find him stupid and boring?"

"That was all before I met him," she said. "One inspired evening. He's been a slug ever since."

Twenty-eight-year-old Diana looked like a *Vogue* cover at each of her twice-weekly visits. The last woman in the world to actually need make-up, she deftly applied it with an artist's hand, and she dressed like the high-fashion model she had once been. Only now the Italian clothes she wore all belonged to her, along with enough gold and diamonds to make me feel she needed a personal security guard as much as a psychiatrist.

I persisted a bit.

"Didn't you tell me that Richard is an active patron of the Modern Museum, that it's not just his checkbook, but that he is *personally* involved in selecting the new acquisitions, . . ."

"Yes . . ."

". . . and that he's taken you all over the world— not just to museums but to the homes of friends he's gathered everywhere . . ."

"Yes, but . . ."

". . . who presumably don't find him stupid and boring?"

"They don't have to *live* with him. It wasn't until I

started to *live* with him that he became stupid and boring."

Diana had been twenty-three when she met Richard, then forty-six and a life-long bachelor. The youngest of nine children, Richard had had to put himself through school. Book learning was a struggle, but once he accepted that he was more inventor than scholar, he never looked back.

Diana, born out of wedlock, did not know her father and was apparently viewed as something of a nuisance by her mother. She was exceedingly bright but, given her "drop dead" beauty, abandoned high school early in favor of modeling full-time. She had soon acquired a cosmopolitan style, the veneer of a good education, and the now five-year live-in relationship with Richard. His pressing her for marriage had precipitated a crisis and her visits to me.

"You were interested enough in Richard for five years. How did his proposal of marriage so change things for you?"

"When I started to think about spending the rest of my life with him, I realized how impossible it would be. Richard is kind, and he loves me and we do interesting things, I guess, but we don't talk to each other. We seem to be good company for everybody else, but when we're alone, *it is deadly*."

"Richard apparently would disagree . . ."

"Richard likes to look at me, dress me, go shopping with me, travel with me, and particularly he likes to ball me. He doesn't need to talk to me."

She raised her wrist and rattled a gold bracelet. "He buys *me* all this exquisite stuff—his taste is impeccable—but never anything for himself. He wears no jewelry, not even a ring. Do you know why? *I'm* his jewelry. He wears *me* on his arm."

"Well, if Richard *were* to try to get past your glittering facade, if he were to try and find out about the *inner you*, what would you want to tell him?''

"Assuming he could hear me—you know, he doesn't listen.''

"Yes, assuming we first cleaned the wax out of his ears, what would you tell him?''

"I would tell him that he's become very dull and that he should try reading. . . .''

"No, I mean, what would you like to tell him about *you*?''

"About me?''

"Yes, about *you*.''

Silence.

"I gather that that is a hard question.''

"Umm. Tell him about me. . . .''

More silence.

I leaned forward, "Pretend *I'm* Richard, I've made my million for the day by 5:00 P.M., I've come home to you, and now I'm all ears. I want to hear about you.''

"You're putting me on the spot. I can't think of anything right now.''

"Nothing? You've been waiting five years to talk to me, and now you have nothing to say?''

"Nothing you'd find interesting.''

"You'd talk to that shrink two hours a week. Why can't you talk to me?''

There was a long pause.

"I can't think of anything significant to talk about at the moment. I . . . I wouldn't want to bore you.''

I put the last question to her gently.

"*You* boring, Diana? I thought *I* was the one who was boring.''

I had never met Richard and so had no way of knowing for sure just how he interacted with Diana. But clearly at least some of her perceptions of him were projections of her own feelings of hollowness. Not that it mattered to Richard—apparently all he required was her glamorous presence. Diana stayed with him—complaining all the while—because *she* needed the affirmation of her worth that his wealth, power, and generous appreciativeness provided; and she knew how to use her beauty and smart-alecky wit to secure it. Richard was more than a lover, a safety net, the father she never had; he was a 360-degree mirror with which she could continuously monitor and affirm her beauty and worth. In turn, she gave him a sense that he was a loving, desirable, valuable man in a way that material wealth never could provide.

Those whose insecurities create a compelling need for validation by others will repeatedly enter into intimate relationships on the basis of their partner's "packaging," expecting it to supply what they feel is missing within themselves. One person may unconsciously choose partners highly regarded for their towering intellect; another strives to select mates who are flamboyantly sexual. A recently wealthy man of lower-class origins might be drawn irresistibly to an elegant society woman; a young girl who doubts her stature and net worth as a person finds herself seeking affirmation through intimacy with a powerful older man. How their lovers appear in the eyes of the world gives them the psychological power to bestow whatever affirmation is so urgently sought.

Validation relationships resound of adolescence, when it seems as if almost everyone desires the captain of the team or the prettiest girl in class. Most adolescents, of course, usually get past such dubious criteria for mate selection as they mature and begin connecting with individuals who fit their deeper, individual psychological processes. But there are some who, like Diana and Richard, become fixed upon the *trappings* of their relationships and remain forever concerned with, "Where will we go tonight?"—"What will we wear?" Constructed almost entirely of appearances, their romance centers around "events" and "things"— perhaps the ski season, an elaborate home, rock concerts, lavish entertaining, exotic vacations. They choose partners according to the sorts of idealized surface criteria one sees in the personal section of the classified (". . . seeking a tall, slim, sensuous, successful . . ."), and they conceive of their relationships as a set of romantic images—a weekend in the country, an evening of champagne by the fire—a television commercial come true.

Because they connect primarily on the basis of superficial Hollywood characteristics, they can look quite good together but have little to talk about. Unable to be real with each other, they fashion a host of distancing maneuvers to ensure that they never get close enough to examine meaningfully either their partner or the reasons for their being together. On those occasions when they risk being critical, they focus on their lover's outer qualities. "You've put on quite a bit of weight lately—you're just letting yourself go."

Buried beneath the glittering role models and polite formality, there is emptiness and often anger. Since they've entered the relationship with the illusion that their mate's accoutrements will remedy their defects and bring happiness, it's not long before they must turn on their lover for letting them down. Bonded to and blinded by external perceptions, they cannot see their problems as residing less in their partner's inevitable failure to deliver the anticipated sorcery, than in their own faulty selection process.

"Deborah's left me again," said Bradford, "and this time it's for good. I've used up my bag of tricks. And yours too, doctor. She says she'll still see you alone, but she's finished with these conjoint sessions."

Deborah had quit teaching school several years after she and Bradford married eight years ago. Public school students seemed to be getting rougher every year, and besides, Bradford made almost as much money in one day practicing surgery as his wife made teaching ninth grade for a month. As she explained during our earlier counseling sessions, she had never really enjoyed teaching but had fallen into it by default.

"Nothing in college had turned me on, particularly. My mother had been a substitute teacher whenever she felt like working, my father couldn't care one way or the other what I did for a living, and there were plenty of job openings at a school two blocks away. It seemed like a respectable place to park myself till I married and had kids of my own."

She was far more particular in what she wanted for a husband.

"All my life I knew I would marry a doctor—a surgeon. And I'm not even Jewish."

"*Any* surgeon?" I asked.

"Of course not. I had to love and respect him. But of all the men I dated over the years, I found it easiest to love and respect doctors. Lawyers were O.K. But a lawyer didn't stand a chance against a doctor."

It was neither the money nor the social status of being "the doctor's wife."

"For me, it was that doctors *care*. A surgeon has your life in his hands. He's been training for a million years to know what to do during those critical moments. He devotes his entire life to the lives of others."

"And perhaps he'd care for you the same way?"

"No, doctor. Don't leap to the obvious. Besides, I'm never sick. But I'd be part of *his* life, of *his* caring for his patients. I'd share that intensity, that devotion.''

At least that was her psyche's theory. A surgeon was the very antithesis of her detached and uninvolved parents.

The reality turned out to be somewhat different. Married to a man who worked fourteen-hour days, most of what she got to share were the 3:00 A.M. phone calls that more often than not summoned Bradford back to the operating room. She acquired in the abstract what she had long coveted, but not a flesh and blood husband.

To his credit, Bradford took Deborah's complaints to heart and tried to do something about them in his studied methodical way.

''I love Deborah. I've never looked at another woman since we met. I don't want to lose her. I cut back on my practice, took long weekends every month just to be together. I learned how to listen better, how to actually *be* with her, but things only got worse. She just doesn't have any feelings for me.''

Bradford had been a gentle but single-minded workaholic. He hadn't time to develop fully as a man or lover, to know *who he was*, other than a topflight student and then a topflight thoracic surgeon. And, he never gave more than superficial consideration to the kind of woman with whom he might be happy.

During their first months, Deborah's intense initial ardor made such enquiry unnecessary. She made efficient use of whatever time they had together, her devotion enabling Bradford partially to break free from a lifelong preoccupation with simply cramming information into his head. Her passionate certainty ignited for the first time his romantic feelings. In turn, eight years later, these feelings galvanized his determination ''to change—to be more the man she wants.''

To no avail.

"He's a fine man just the way he is," she said. "It's just that he seems so . . . limited. I feel so very sad, and very sorry. There's nothing wrong with him. He gave me what I thought I wanted. Only it's not enough. What I want now—who I want now—is very different."

Turns out who she wanted now was the nationally famous plastic surgeon who did her breasts.

"I know my own heart, doctor. There's no going back."

I saw Deborah and Bradford individually, Deborah for another two months, Bradford for the greater part of a year, helping them find the least painful and most constructive way of ending their marriage. As the focus on "our marriage" faded, each began to look at the emotional needs that had led them to choose a relationship essentially empty at its core. They learned something about the kind of people they had been and had now become, and about those with whom they might best be able to build a solidly grounded and lasting relationship in the future.

I specifically selected Diana and Richard and Bradford and Deborah to illustrate the *validation relationship* because both couples express in a singular, unalloyed way the particular drive that leads people to choose lovers primarily on the basis of surface personality traits and social roles—to inevitably disappointing effect. Though there's always a little "validating" going on initially within almost all romantic bonds, contributing greatly to the immediate chemistry (and doubtless fueling those "love at first sight" experiences), it is only when partners are able to travel further and find or create a number of other, sound bridges between their respective inner selves that their relationship can deepen, grow, and endure.

Doing It Better

The power (and ultimately the hazard) of the validating relationship lies in its ability to enhance and shore up self-worth. At its best, it teaches us important, heretofore hidden things about our inner selves. At its worst, it robs us of autonomy.

The key to avoiding obsessive dependence upon one's lover for ego-boosting revelations is to find ways to incorporate the support and insight offered into one's basic sense of self. Instruction replaces addiction. In that way, esteem can be maintained even if the relationship ends. Relinquish to others the power to affirm that you are O.K., and you remain dependent on your intimate connections to them. But if you absorb your lover's validating message, you are on your way to becoming self-validating and far less needy of a validation fix again and again from someone else.

Thus, "I must be bright and beautiful because this dazzling man has chosen *me*," becomes "I know I'm bright and beautiful because I've learned to listen to and hear my clever thoughts, because I've paid attention to the way I look when I voice them, and because *I* hear and see myself as he does." In short, you work toward taking in what the validation mirror reflects and then remembering what you saw. Though initially using the relationship to lend support in those areas you feel deficient, you then *grab hold of that validation and keep it for yourself*.

So, should your splendiferous lover, the king (or queen) of Rumania, startle you with a validating assurance that you are positively the most charming person in the kingdom and he (she) cannot live without you, he (she) has gifted you with a first-class opportunity to tell yourself: "Well, if Rumanian royalty, with access to anyone in the country, says these things, they must be true, because they ought to know. Now let's see if *I* can locate, within myself, the things they say they perceive in me.''

Paradoxically, the more you feel and behave in a certain way—bright, attractive, or whatever—the more people respond to you as a bright or attractive person. You develop a reinforcing process that is a sort of validation relationship in reverse: Rather than using validation as a way of becoming a certain kind of person, your becoming a certain kind of person brings validation.

However inordinate the needs that hook us into validating relationships, we come by them honestly—they are quite simply a product of the home in which we grew up. It is eminently reasonable that a woman raised in a household where females were depreciated might be drawn to men whose principal strength is their ability to at least make her feel good about her femininity. Children never allowed to feel as smart as their parents or siblings not unexpectedly later tend to choose lovers along side whose dim powers of cerebration they appear as brilliant stars.

But validation relationships pose an insoluble dilemma: If you choose a lover consistent primarily with your aspirations rather than with where you actually are in your development (but who allows you to shine in *his* or *her* reflected glory), you will always feel vaguely one down. On the other hand, the repeated choice of one whose only significant virtue lies in making you look terrific soon brings boredom and frustration as well as stifled growth. For that reason, however compelling their initial chemistry, validation relationships must ultimately be abandoned. In the interim, however, no harm comes from letting a relationship help you feel good about yourself through its calling attention to attributes previously unrecognized.

But your validating lover can play a much more important role in your life than just giving you strokes or
temporarily filling in the potholes in your self-esteem:
for this relationship can teach you about your undis-
covered but enduring value as a person and can provide indelible, lasting instruction about heretofore
unappreciated elements of who you are. So listen to
your lover and believe what he or she says. Several
such profoundly educational experiences can prepare
you for new, very different kinds of relationships.

Structure-Building Relationships— Constructing a Framework

"We are *more* than husband and wife," Jane said
quietly. "Jack and I are best friends."

And indeed they were. They cared for, respected,
admired one another. What they no longer had with
one another was much of a sex life, a deficiency now
threatening their twenty-three-year marriage and bringing them to me for counseling.

I asked them when and how they met, and why, of
all the people they knew and might have picked, they
chose to marry each other.

"We grew up together," said Jack. "We even went
to the same grade school."

"We were the same height back then—real short,"
added Jane, "and they always sat us at adjacent desks
near the front of the class. We lived maybe three
blocks apart and always walked home together. We
went on to the same high school and the same junior
college."

"And we went to Sunday school together," said
Jack.

"I ate dinner more at Jack's house than my own—
my Mom was never into cooking . . ."

"She has this great recipe for fish in catsup sauce," Jack chimed in.

"I never thought . . . it never occurred to me to marry anyone else. For years Jack and I were inseparable. Who else was I supposed to marry?"

So they wedded at nineteen, bought a small house with a little help from both their parents, had the requisite two children, saved for and purchased a larger home, and saw their children go off to the same high school they had attended and then on to college. They prospered; they were content. But gradually they had ceased to see each other in a sexual way.

"Jane hasn't wanted to have sex in over a month now."

"Come on Jack. Don't put it all on me. The past few years you've shown more enthusiasm for Mom's cooking than for my body."

"I love your body. Your body's just fine. I . . . I admit . . . I guess I'm just not very turned on these days . . ."

"I'll say you're not. A couple of months ago, doctor, I ordered one of those lacey black things from this Victoria's Secret catalog, put it on . . ."

". . . and he didn't notice?"

"Oh, he noticed. He laughed at me."

"Yeah, well—just a little," said Jack. "I mean, you're my *wife* Jane, not some hooker."

Structure-building relationships are unconsciously but no less deliberately designed to *rear the partners*. Established typically between two people just beyond adolescence (or between older people who first took ten years to develop a career), they are characterized by a close *external* fit and common history. They are age appropriate, and are usually formed by people of comparable socioeconomic status and educational levels.

Often they evolve into or are part and parcel of "a good first marriage."

The structure-building relationship is future oriented. The couple works hard for tomorrow—for the dream house, the children. They typically put their inner lives, emotional growth, and personal satisfaction "on hold" in the service of an idealized marital framework or family. For a decade or two, they busily live out scripts written by their families of origin. All this takes place by tacit mutual consent. Contentment reigns.

But because they are focused on concrete goals and tasks, couples in structure-building relationships can become rather asexual after the first few years, with much of their passion going into growing up and shouldering burdens together. Commitment is more to family than to each other or even to themselves. Individual preferences and values are ruthlessly subordinated to "the relationship," often with the children as the primary focus. The couple relates to each other more as *parents* of their children than as *partners* in intimacy, and they make even less time to appreciate each other as husband and wife (though ever more tempted by the possibilities for sexual gratification outside the marriage).

Some such couples get past these hazards and remain close as the years pass, but others become simultaneously dependent and competitive in a sibling rivalry way. Though sharing a lifestyle and many cultural values, they are increasingly out of sync psychologically, and they find they have even greater difficulty entering into cooperative ventures or even playing together. They may try keeping the peace by having separate "domains"—perhaps she stays in the kitchen or garden, he remains in the den or "back at the office." But conflict grows, with resolution poor due to diminishing areas of commonality and contact. Their need to fight with each other to establish who they are as individuals increases, and the underlying power struggles become even more draining. Eventually, a great number of these marriages are reduced to a strained friendship. For some, all that is left are the fights, punctuating the silence.

In Jack and Jane's case, there was no lack of sexual skills; neither had there been any diminishment in their more than two decades of mutual devotion. What had happened simply was that they had successfully completed their marital process. Just as children who were once best friends are unlikely to have much in common in their thirties, Jack and Jane, though starting out with near identical aspirations and plans, no longer had a romantic basis on which to continue.

Twenty-three years ago they had made an implicit contract, less to stay bonded "till death do us part," than to build a structure in which they could grow and raise themselves and their family. They had now fulfilled its terms. It was time to move on. "Treatment" for them evolved from the *sex therapy* initially sought into *divorce counseling* to help bring their long, fruitful relationship to a gentle, dignified end.

Terry and Miles' structure-building had been even more literal. Terry's father had left them two dry cleaning stores. By the sixth year of their marriage, they had expanded their business into a nationwide chain of specialty cleaners and were on the verge of branching out into Europe and parts of Asia.

"We have the financing, and then some," said Terry. "Miles made a dozen trips to Japan this past year and locked in a solid Japanese connection. We're gonna be the first to crack the market. We're all set. But . . ."

"But . . ." added Miles.

"But what?"

Terry spoke quietly. "I'm not so sure we should be doing it *together*. Miles and me."

"It won't work any other way," said Miles.

"I know," said Terry. "But I'm afraid of what will happen to us when everything does start to work."

Terry and Miles related well to each other as business partners. Closely attuned to each other's thinking, they could work long, mutually productive hours together.

"We both want the same thing," Terry continued. "Business comes naturally to both of us. And where I'm weak, Miles is strong. I give great phone but hate to travel. He actually *enjoys* airline food but gets an earache from telephone receivers. But we *both* understand what needs to be done. And neither of us ever has to explain why dinner has to be kept warm in the oven for another two hours."

But in the process of empire building, Miles and Terry were rapidly losing sight of each other. More and more they were just business partners, less and less were they husband and wife, and almost never lovers. So they decided to do something very difficult—difficult because both of them had an enormous investment in the status quo.

"Frankly, we get off on the pressure. We like making money," said Terry.

"And we like the idea of someday being worldwide big shots," said Miles. "But we like the idea of staying married even more."

So they put the invasion of Japan on hold and created an independent division to set up plants in Europe. They cut into profits and hired two extra people to man the phones, and even found someone else who liked "steak or chicken" to carry some of the traveling. Then they took up bowling, enrolled together in an art class, and just last month cashed in a large chunk of

Miles' frequent flyer mileage for a Baltic cruise. In short, they stopped adding to structure and instead created the time and space to live happily within it.

Terry and Miles are seen as a marital success, while couples like Jack and Jane mistakenly look back on their experience as a "failed marriage." In fact, the latter marriage also achieved exactly what it was "designed," psychologically speaking, to do. Of course, we want all such marriages to continue, evolving into something new and more appropriate once structure-building is completed. And many couples do indeed effect these kinds of changes, relating to each other in middle age very differently, perhaps, than the ways that fit so well when they first connected, but with no less gratification. A unique quality of the romantic process is its degree of adaptability and capacity to metamorphosize.

But just as peach trees are not a "failed species" because they live on average only twenty-five years when apple trees typically survive to a hundred, the contribution that a structure-building marriage makes to the family that has evolved around it is no less, simply because its dimensions are finite. Completion may mean an end, but it also marks a beginning.

Doing It Better

If your present relationship is primarily a structure-building one, the comfort and security you are presently enjoying can make it difficult to spot the sources of concurrent discontentments, or potentially more serious future dissatisfactions. Although awareness that the relationship isn't working well anymore can be quite acute, because you are surrounded by so much that is valuable it's often difficult to know what to do to change what no longer fits for you without disrupting all the good parts as well.

In my experience, the singular down side of the structure-building relationship is that it fosters the repeated choice of reliability over excitement and joy, and trades satisfaction in the moment for possible future returns. It follows, then, that the revitalization of a structure-building relationship requires, instead, taking a few risks—today.

Begin by making a list of the things you've always wanted to do with your life but haven't done, and then, with each item, ask yourself what stopped you. In truth, could you not do many of these things *right now*? Is there something inherent in being a husband/wife/parent that gets in the way, or is the obstacle just you? Do you really need the permission or cooperation of others? Does it really require that much money? Have you not imposed upon *yourself* a life of quiet deprivation?

Often this sort of unflinching enquiry will reveal that it is only inertia or perhaps the "safe" clinging to role stereotypes that has held you back, stopping you from taking those trips, or setting aside time to write poetry, or going back to school, or joining a choral group or a Sierra Club wilderness expedition. The solution is obvious: Take the first decisive step toward living *your* life as opposed merely to carrying out a structured spousal or parental role. Give priority to getting more of what you want for yourself—*now*. If you always put things off and live only for the future, your entire life will be a dress rehearsal.

Even a relationship seemingly built entirely of bricks and mortar can blossom into excitement and passion if both of you learn to *tune into each other's feelings*—particularly feelings that are *not* task related. "I worry about junior" or, "I'm anxious about our taking out an equity loan on the house" certainly are feelings that should be communicated, but these have less power to renew a relationship than talking about "getting sad sometimes about all the compromises I must live with at work" or asking whether your partner also "feels all alone sometimes even when we're together."

Whatever the sentiments expressed, don't rush to reassurance or solutions, thereby cutting off emotions along with the psychological changes and growth that might follow. Feelings are worth revealing even when they do not lead to concrete remedies. In bringing emotions back into a structure-building relationship, problems shared are at least as important as problems solved.

It is especially difficult for people in structure-building relationships to entirely put aside *problems* for a while in favor of *play*. But it can be done (just don't work too hard at doing it). Try making a point of interrupting the comfort of certainty with the arousal of surprise. Show up at home—or at each other's offices—for lunch, and then skip lunch. Or take off somewhere together for two days mid-week (or send the kids on a weekend holiday). Take a community college course together in a potentially new area of interest outside of each other's expertise. Try for something different and unexpected in bed, such as a week's commitment to "anything and everything except intercourse"—now *that* should introduce new levels of excitement.

Finally, it is my experience that the structure-building relationship can be particularly lethal for women with no money of their own, and thereby entirely dependent on their mates for support. Financial dependence is a sure road to psychological impotence. It's hard to take charge of one's life without at least a modest independent income. Even in the home, as elsewhere, money is power. For that reason, I think it important that, whenever possible, women maintain separate bank accounts and that both partners have work outside home-making responsibilities, even if the family's needs do not require two breadwinners. There is no dearth of useful things one can do part-time to generate a little income, and the money earned need not be equal to that of your partner for it to earn emotional equity.

Experimental Relationships—Finding What Fits

Harvey yawned.

"Sorry, doc. Nothing personal. I was partying all night."

"With Sarah?"

"Sarah was last week. This was Mary."

"I'm starting to lose track. Wasn't Mary last week?"

"You're thinking of Marie. First it was Marie, then Sarah, now Mary."

"I've got it. I think. How did you meet Mary?"

"Sarah introduced us. Mary is Sarah's sister."

"Sarah's *sister?* You're dating two sisters?"

"They are very different."

"How does Sarah feel about your dating her sister?"

"She doesn't know."

"She will."

And too bad. I had started to like Sarah, the first woman Harvey had dated long enough for me to get some sense of person—a solid-seeming sort with whom he might at last have the semblance of an enduring relationship.

"No she won't," Harvey assured me. "Mary feels too guilty to tell her, and she swore *me* to secrecy. So I'll be seeing them both, I guess. Besides, I don't see why I should have to give up either one just because they're sisters."

Harvey was certainly making up for lost time. He had gone from college directly into a ten-year marriage during which he was—in his words—"oppressively monogamous." Recently, in quick succession, he had obtained a law degree and a position as house counsel for a large pharmaceutical firm, had summarily ended his marriage by means of a cataclysmic affair with his secretary, and had then loosed his long-suppressed libido upon the entire unsuspecting female population of San Francisco. He saw older women, teenage women, married women, a lesbian nurse, a Hispanic prison guard, a Malaysian stripper, a former law school professor, and, not least and certainly not last, an ex-nun. He bought condoms by the case, using them diligently (except with the ex-nun who reportedly deplored even health precautions if they smacked of contraception). He was an equal opportunity seducer, and although all of his relationships with women concluded rather badly, he had such a good time in the interim, they were more than worth it. The means justified the ends.

Lest you think Harvey's adventures merely those of the stereotypic male sowing his oats, I should hasten to add that, in many ways, his psychodynamics were not unlike those of a middle-aged woman I treated briefly some years earlier. This managing editor of a West Coast magazine was what she called, "too happy," hardly the usual reason for which people turn to psychiatry but one which, nonetheless, had raised for her some serious concerns. As she put it:

"I was married for nineteen years. I raised three children, two of whom now have children of their own. I was president of the P.T.A. I taught Sunday school for as long as I can remember. How can I now be so happy, divorced, and living in a *ménage à trois?*"

Let us explore the historical reasons people repeatedly enter into "unusual" or unlikely relationships, and the substantial power of such experimentation. Ideally, during our adolescence we utilize a fair number of instructive, relatively short-term romances or near-romances in the service of maturation and of establishing who we are in relation to others. Often, however, such experimentation is culturally denied or deferred in favor of developing a new career, entering an early marriage, or raising a family. If so, then typically during the third or fourth decades of life or perhaps after the end of a first marriage, experimentation more age-appropriate to the twenties or late teens may be vigorously resumed. For relatively young people, an experimental relationship can extend over several years, but for older ones, who presumably learn faster, they are usually quite brief—sometimes just one-night stands. (Many extramarital affairs are, in fact, experimental relationships.)

For some, experimentation is very nearly a lifelong process, either because they are uniquely slow learners in this arena or because they are always finding more to learn. A point can be reached, however, when what appears to be experimentation is, in fact, the settling into a rigid, fixed pattern, wherein change itself becomes the constant.

I am acquainted with a group of sixteen individuals arranged around such unremitting experimentation. All but three of the members are office workers in a large West Coast insurance corporation. Included in the sixteen are six married couples; the other four participants share a large condominium and a four-cornered, stable romantic relationship. All sixteen meet two nights a week. Several times a year, they break up into smaller groups and go on vacations with each other. But what makes these sixteen people most unusual, besides their congeniality, durability of friendship, commonality of interests, and obvious devotion to each other, is the virtual absence of any sexual barriers between them. They all regularly have sex with each others' partners.

Joanie put her group's sentiments well: "We do genuinely love each other. And loving one person fully, generously, seems to add to our capacity to love others fully. Once you've opened up the passion within you, it becomes a force—a kind of energy that spreads out, touching and involving those around you. More and more people turn on to you, and you turn on to them. We're never bored sexually and never have to take energy away from our primary relationships to sneak around outside the group. It's a larger system than most people enjoy, but it is a *closed* system."

Closed to a variety of potential intruders as well. "We've all been AIDS tested. There's been no sexually transmitted diseases in any of us since we all got together. We have no sexual secrets. We don't need them. You don't have to hide part of yourself from people who think that you're a good person just the way you are."

What Joanie and her friends have created is an epidemiologically safe, rather unorthodox matrix within which their romantic relationships are kept at the experimental level. In all probability, however, in time any number of them may find that instead of stimulating evolution and development, such sexual variety holds individuals in place. Repeating the same experiment again and again may have its rewards, but growth is not one of them.

Though experimental relationships usually do not involve much forward motion, they can be an informative kind of treading water. They can also move sideways;

they may even be regressive. Whatever their direction or speed, their distinguishing characteristics are that each is very different from previous romantic experiences, each is probably quite different from those to follow, and, once the data have been gathered, they all end—usually in fairly short order. Though often exciting and instructive, they don't seem to lead anywhere. Once we have completed the protocol and learned whatever that experiment was designed to teach, we move on.

Doing It Better

There are few subjects that have received as much literary attention as love and romance. Yet even the best read of us must start our experiences from scratch. We are all obliged *personally* to complete certain trial and error processes if we are to find out what the meaning of love is for *ourselves*. For this purpose, brief experimental relationships are inordinately useful. Permanence in itself is small virtue. I know of plenty of long-term relationships that rely heavily upon the partners' emotionally draining capacity to *perform*, to be somebody else in the service of staying together. Such relationships endure because of mutual dependency, fear of being alone, a masochistic penchant for hardship, or intense passivity that is mistaken for compromise. By contrast, the intensity of joy in many experimental relationships, though short-lived, can be an eminently rational basis for assessing its true value. A ten-day tumultuous, soul-searing encounter at a critical moment may contribute more to your development than a ten-year marriage.

As we mature, most of us will try on several experimental relationships, partial or complete, some consummated, many not, and even a few lived just in fantasy—the strength of compelling fictional characters and of good love stories is in their power to carry us along in our imagination, fostering experimentation within the safety of our own minds.

On the other hand, it is possible to get stuck at an experimental level, particularly when you need to master an especially tough, unyielding lesson. Though experimentation is sometimes the fastest way to gather important data about yourself, if you seem to be "learning" the same lesson over and over again or you experience emotional pain—recurrent emotional pain—the time has come to stop. "Just say no" to potential partners, and spend several months *alone* reflecting on what you have been doing, why you have been doing it, and where you are going—forward, upward, backward, in circles, or whatever. As the psychic dust settles a bit, you should be better able to inventory your recent experiences and make more accurate judgments about which ones came closest to working for you. You will thereby provide yourself some direction when you set out to try again.

Avoidance Relationships—Playing It Safe

Philippa was a stewardess for a foreign carrier with a base in San Francisco. To outward appearances, she had it all—travel and adventure, access to men in every (air)port, entrée at boutiques worldwide, and the face and figure of a lovely thirty-year-old woman who had in fact just turned forty, an event that had sent her to me in a panic.

"I have the strange suspicion that I look as young as I do because I spend half my life suspended—up in the air. Were I ever to settle down on earth, I'd instantly decay. British Airways is my Shangri-la. If I ever left them, I would not just suddenly look my age, I'd turn to dust. So I've got to keep flying."

"I take it flying has lost its glamour."

"No, I actually love it. I've got twenty years seniority. Any flights I want. The problem is, I don't know what *else* to do. I don't know what it would be like to spend four consecutive weeks on the ground. I don't know what it would be like to spend four consecutive weeks with one man."

"You play the field?"

"Not really. Not anymore. I really just see three men: one in London, one in San Francisco, and one— a pilot—whenever we're working the same flight. It's just that every date with each of these guys is a *first* date. Maybe a second. We seem to get into something, start getting somewhere, then I take off on a trip. I come back a couple of weeks later, and we start again at the beginning. I've been dating one of these men for fifteen years and still haven't gotten past that second date. We've even had the same argument for fifteen years. *That's* what's not fun anymore. And *that's* what I do not know how to change. I haven't a clue."

Philippa led a breathless life, one seemingly crowded with relationships, whereas in fact she used relationships as she used her career—to *avoid* connecting. Involved with several, she was intimate with none. On her fortieth birthday, Philippa had an anxiety attack when she realized that she was, indeed, alone.

Harry, also, was alone, as was his wife, even though they ate and slept under the same roof, had sex an average of three times a week, and enjoyed the same T.V. programs—*a lot* of T.V. programs. In fact, they were infinitely closer to the characters in "Dallas" than to each other. Other than a mutual interest in the overwrought misadventures of favored television persona, they had little in common. They had drifted into and remained in their marriage because it provided a comfortable, undemanding status quo, and it relieved them of having truly to interact with others. They each had their jobs, and anything else they wanted was right there in the bedroom, in front of the tube. Marriage and CBS kept them together. They never had to risk being close.

Then, one evening, Harry must have decided he wanted something more—or at least something different—because during the eleven o'clock news, he went out for a carton of yogurt and never came back.

Connie hid her avoidance mechanisms in workaholism. She put in a sixty- to seventy-hour week as editor for a small biogenetic firm where she was responsible for every word that was to see print—reports to the FDA, grant applications, quarterly financial statements, and so on. It was high-pressure, deadline work, with each deadline succeeded by another. Home provided no respite—if she wasn't at her personal word processor until three in the morning, she'd be on the phone to one associate or another, "working things out." Obsessed with verbal clarity, she wrote and re-wrote. No sentence was safe from her perfectionism until actually on the printed page.

"I'm a mediocre writer but a sterling re-writer. Eventually, my syntax is entirely in order," she assured me, "even if my personal life is not."

And indeed, things were not well between Connie and her husband, Mac. As he explained: "If she's not actually at work, she's thinking about work. She'll awaken from a sound sleep, get out of bed, and re-write. On more than one occasion, we've been making love and I can tell her mind is editing a report or something. I have to take her backpacking in the sticks where there's no electricity or phones, or to Mexico where the phones don't really work, and keep her there for three or four days to get her turned back into a normal woman who relates. The rest of the time, no mat-

ter where her body is, her head is on the job.
Sometimes I wonder why she married me. She already
had a husband.''

Connie was herself well aware of the degree to
which work had become an addiction that had taken
over her life, and she was now ready to try a solution
she and Mac had talked about for months. She gave up
her job where the demands on her time by her
employer and her own obsessive psyche seemed without limit, in favor of casual, part-time work at home.
She still accepted occasional projects in her new capacity as ''consultant'' to her old boss, but mostly, she
freelanced.

For several months, it seemed to work. She found
time to read fiction, get a tan, do some fancy cooking.
She even joined in Mac's twice-weekly poker games.
But it wasn't long before her new clients' manuscripts
and drafts were creeping out of her little office onto the
dining room table, then spreading to the living room,
and finally, metastasizing to the bedroom. Stacks of
papers, printouts, and files around the bed soon made
it difficult, both literally and figuratively, for either
Connie or Mac to get into it. Within half a year of
leaving her regular job, Connie had arranged a ninety-
hour workweek for herself. Once again, at one or two
in the morning, despite her husband's plaintive pleas to
join him in the bedroom, she'd be wedded to some
article or book. She had quickly slipped back into her
old ways: *better read than bed*.

Both Connie's need to avoid intimacy and the workaholism with which she fulfilled that need were readily
traceable to hypercritical, high-achieving parents who
metered out their few words of praise for *what* Connie
could achieve, never for *who* she was. Connie grew up
convinced that she could win respect and admiration
for her *accomplishments*, but risking *interpersonal inti-*

macy was a much dicier proposition and, in her mind, more likely to bring indifference or rejection than acceptance and love.

Avoidant relationships are founded on a need to escape feelings of vulnerability or loss, emotional commitment, or threats to self-esteem. Characterized by distance, busyness, superficiality, secretiveness, denial, withholding, and mistrust, such relationships can form in time of need, crisis, fear, or emotional depletion or can be part of an on-going, lifelong pattern. They provide safe havens—partners in avoidant relationships needn't ever change, mature, or even feel.

People relating at this level often impulsively choose partners who are incongruous with them across the board—in personal style, emotional rhythm, intelligence, socioeconomic status, in even age and gender—and then employ mechanisms such as job demands or frequent but impersonal sex to distract themselves from forming a meaningful connection. Fights are common because of the serviceability of conflict in maintaining distance.

Avoidant relationships can start and end quite abruptly and often unannounced. They can be recurrent and intermittent. There are few formal boundaries. Even among the long-married the nature of this connection is rarely articulated, while unmarried lovers often simply "run into each other" and just as casually disappear from each other's lives.

Doing It Better

All of us probably have had some difficulty finding that optimum distance between ourselves and our romantic intimates. We each have different notions of how much *togetherness/being alone* is best. (Indeed, a useful screening test question for a future enduring relationship might be: Do I feel as comfortable and unintruded upon when with this wonderful person hour after hour as I do when I'm alone?

As we draw ever nearer to our partners, it becomes necessary to devise mechanisms for being alone and separate (or, at least, protective of our own personal space) while simultaneously maintaining that special connection. Some devices are better than others: Getting caught up in an engrossing novel from time to time sounds like a good one; regularly tuning the other person out or getting stoned or drunk are probably less happy choices. But when being together depends primarily upon a long, deadening series of avoidance maneuvers (or when the partners have drastically disparate convictions as to what constitutes a comfortable distance between them), the relationship can fly apart through its own centrifugal force.

Avoidant partners typically come from families wherein any individuation is labeled a rejection of family values. As children they were expected always to subordinate their personal needs to those of "the family"; as adults they find they can only honor themselves in private, isolated from their important relationships. In addition, these families are suffused with the conviction that all personal feelings are inherently and ultimately painful or dangerous; the children learn to keep their feelings buried so deeply that as adults they are utterly unable to tolerate any expression of emotion.

It is my experience that most people predisposed in this fashion to avoidant relationships are compelled to escape intimacy because of their inability to set limits *within* a romantic framework. In order to maintain their autonomy and avoid emotional overload, they run away, the only device by which they can sustain a sense of self. If they could learn a way to maintain some apartness *within* their intimate relationships, they would have less reason to perpetually disappear.

If any of this sounds like an echo of your own family experiences or of your relationship patterns, you might want to measure candidly just how much you do enjoy being alone—being totally in charge with no need to compromise or expose your areas of emotional vulnerability—and to look at just how far you're willing to go to remain separate. Do you regularly avoid the difficult task of setting limits within your intimate relationships and simply walk away when the going gets rough or your partner feels intrusive? Do you deliberately choose lovers whose uncommon skill at back-pedaling gets the job done for you? If so, the next question is, "What am I afraid of?" If you gravitate toward fleet-footed lovers, ask, "What am I afraid will happen if he/she stops running and I really got everything I've been asking for?"

I have found that the hardest task for those predisposed to an avoidance pattern is in identifying and then choosing less elusive partners, and/or in abandoning favorite escapist tricks. Begin by developing an early warning system about intense but determinedly unavailable, inveterate bachelors/bachelorettes. (Although most of us have answering machines these days, he/she should be home on occasion to answer the phone personally; and although we all live crowded lives, his/her availability on several successive evenings should not always lie utterly outside the realm of possibility.) See if you can recognize when *your* Houdini persona comes to the fore, and then try sitting on it and just staying put for a while longer. You may discover less Draconian ways of achieving some distance and space than fleeing the planet. Try establishing parameters for privacy *within* the relationship, perhaps requiring that your partner leave you absolutely alone two or three hours every day. Perhaps you can have your own room or even just part of a room that is *absolutely yours*.

If you set limits *within* the relationship, creating space and privacy for yourself inside its boundaries, you'll have less reason for either you or your partner to take off. Learn to recognize the first stage of the avoidant process—when you suddenly find yourself intensely negative, relentlessly finding problems for every solution—and take hold of the situation before it takes hold of you. Finally, whenever you feel yourself tempted to bolt down the road, ask yourself: "What's the real risk here? Is this trip really necessary?"

Fusion Relationships—Trying to Stand

If avoidance is one side of the coin, fusion is the other.

Sally and Hal both were on their third marriage, and this one was quickly going the way of the other two. This time, however, there was a difference: Sally had had a child by Hal and was pregnant with another. So the couple was sent by the family court for mandatory predissolution counseling—a last and rather anachronistic court-ordered effort to "save the marriage."

"There's no marriage to save," said Hal with some insight. "She's five months pregnant and still runs out on me at night."

"I don't 'run out on you.' I visit with friends."

"All your 'friends' are down in the bar. And they're all men."

"What the hell is wrong with a few drinks with friends? So what if they are men? *You're* working all night. What the hell am I supposed to do, sit home and crochet?"

"You're going to have a goddamn baby! Stay home and prepare for the baby!"

"What do you mean 'prepare'? Start the water boiling? This is the twentieth century, you know. Pregnant women can have normal lives . . ."

"You see what I mean, doc? Sally, what a goddamn rationalization! You leave a woman alone for a little while and she'll screw around on you. It's not normal to be sitting night after night in a bar . . ."

"You didn't mind it when you met me. Seems to me you were pretty much a fixture there yourself 'til you went on graveyard."

And so he had been. He had met his two previous wives in much the same way and married them within a month. Not much later, he had divorced them.

There are those for whom *anyone's* company is better than none at all. As bespeaks their fuzzy boundaries and markedly underdeveloped sense of self, such people—whose greatest fear is being alone—will tolerate adultery, beatings, and other massive blows to self-esteem and will go to any lengths to bind their partners to them. They quickly form intense relationships in which they long for intimacy yet fear it because of the challenge it poses to their fragile sense of autonomy. Neither closeness nor distance feels comfortable. In many instances, their relationships do not last the year. When on occasion one does endure, it is destructively symbolic—two half-persons fusing together to try to make a single whole one.

These *fusion relationships* are characterized by a clinging dependency alternated with hostile impulsiveness, and by a single-minded, controlling possessiveness, sometimes to the exclusion of anyone or anything else. Partners view any suggestion of a wish to be separate, as a threat, yet really have little in common save mutual fear and their relatively uniformed ego structures. They can marry two weeks after they meet and divorce two months later. Dissolution is rarely constructive and sometimes quite violent.

Mike and his live-in girlfriend, Milly, also came to me by way of the courts, but for a very different reason. Mike had beaten Milly severely on two occasions, and for him it was either psychotherapy or jail. Mike had voluntarily sought counseling; Mike was there in lieu of incarceration and Milly came to his sessions because I had asked her to come and had promised not to leave her alone with her boyfriend without her express consent.

"I'm terrified of him, doctor. If I wasn't home when he came in from work, if I wanted to visit some friends or do a little extra unscheduled shopping, if I'd try doing anything on my own, he'd get furious. He can beat the s--- out of me."

"Yet, you stay," I observed.

"No. After he slaps me around, I split. If a man lays a hand on me, that's it."

"But you come back."

"He finds *me*. He tracks me down and he begs and he's sweet and loving and cries those crocodile tears . . ."

"What crocodile tears?" Mike shouted, almost out of his chair. "You know damn well I love you. I don't want to live without you . . ."

I interrupted. "You wouldn't think you'd want to beat up on someone you love and can't live without. Maybe *that's* Mike's problem, or should I say, *both* your problems. If Mike didn't feel he needed you so badly, if he didn't feel you were so much a part of him, he wouldn't have to guard you so closely."

"She sure likes the sex," Mike asserted. "There's no fooling there."

"I shouldn't let you do it, especially after you've hit me."

"Tell me you don't like it."

"I shouldn't let you . . ."

But she always did. Milly had as big a problem with boundaries and with separation as did Mike. Their repetitive, painful drama was based on a collaborative script. Each felt too threatened by the other to live comfortably together, yet neither could tolerate being apart. *To be apart meant being alone*.

Things improved superficially for Mike and Milly by the end of our third session. They even left holding hands, despite my admonition that it was too soon for them to be getting close again. Two days later, Milly was in the hospital with a fractured skull, and Mike was behind bars. As soon as she was well enough, Milly visited Mike at the county jail every day.

There are probably seeds of a fusion relationship in us all—moments when we feel incomplete without somebody else in our lives, when we define ourselves a bit too closely around another person. Nobody has parents so perfect or a childhood so fortuitous that he or she springs forth as a wholly formed, self-reliant person with never a need to lean on others. But there are a most unfortunate few others who emerge from adolescence with the conviction that any competence they may have as individuals is limited to their ability to find and meld with another. Being a separate and distinct person means to be alone, and alone means to be lonely, empty, abandoned. They do not connect with others to enrich their lives but only to survive.

There is worthwhile instruction buried here for all of us, if hard for some of us to accept: *though being alone and bereft of love can certainly bring sadness and an intense longing for restoration of our previous intimate connections or for immediate creation of new ones, being alone is also critical to preparations for a fresh start with someone quite different*. People who always bounce from one relationship instantly to another are probably just running in place.

Doing It Better

Ultimately, the best medicine I know of for those prone to fusion relationships is "tincture of time"—and the maturity that (usually) comes with it. It is no coincidence that, in my counseling practice, most of those enmeshed in fusion relationships are adolescents (although, admittedly, I've counseled not a few "adolescents" who will never see thirty again, but who suffered such psychological abuse as children that they were left with the insecurities and fuzzy ego boundaries that normally characterize many younger people). In the meantime, maintaining a diversity of relationships and interests is essential if one is to escape being swallowed up by romance.

The hallmark of the fusion couple is their isolation from anyone but each other and from everything else going on around them. All their attention and energy is focused on the relationship. Friendships, school, work, parents are totally subordinate to the all-consuming love affair. If you suspect you are caught up in this kind of process, your best defense is to maintain those other connections and activities. Eschew Vince Lombardi—it's perilous enough that your love affair is *everything* to you without its also being the *only* thing in your life. Learn to back off, to take time out before things become intolerably intense. In fact, the best time to make some space for yourself is precisely when the relationship is feeling awfully good. The more obsessive the bonding, the more benefits will accrue from a little cordial distancing and balance. Stay involved with the rest of your life. Keep committed to the other people who have been important to you, some of whom may provide perspective and favorably dilute your primary relationship.

If you can pull away for a moment, you might be able to figure out what is distinctive in your relationship that makes it so compelling. You may find, for example, that you are addicted less to your lover than to what emerges from yourself in his or her company, the persona he or she brings out. In short, who *you* seem to become when you are with your lover is more important to you than your lover himself.

Perhaps all your life you've wished you were witty. He insists that you are, laughing at even your least impressive turns of phrase. So you feel witty in his company, and it is this witty persona that gets you hooked.

Or perhaps you are addicted to your partner's implied promise of what the future will bring if you stay in the relationship, that although things may be tense now, it will work out wonderfully and the two of you will ride off into the sunset together. You are snared on the future because it's so easy to go along with the promises. Simply aspiring to Nirvana is far more seductive than the hard relationship work necessary to achieve it.

So reconnect with the *real* world. Focus again on your health, job, checkbook balance, even dental care. Work towards maintaining elements of a separate life of your own. Another person can never meet all of your needs, however much he/she may love you and however hard he/she tries. Their inevitable failure to do so should not be taken as a statement about either his/her feelings for you or your intrinsic loveability.

Healing Relationships—Binding the Wounds

It had been a murderous divorce for Isabel. The loss of her husband of twenty-seven years, her status, and her home had left her shattered and immobilized with despair.

"I thought we were happy. In fact we *were* happy. Irving simply changed. Only he didn't bother to let me in on it."

"You didn't see it coming?" I asked.

"We had just come back from two marvelous weeks in Curacao, one of our best vacations ever. We had a terrific time. Irving was his usual bantering, loving self. I see now that he was giving the condemned prisoner her last meal, so he made sure I had whatever I wanted . . ."

Her eyes reddened. She paused to collect herself.

"I spent more than half my life with that man, half my life as 'Isabel and Irving,' as 'Mrs. Irving Schneider.' I do not know how to be *just Isabel*."

In the months following Irving's announcement that he no longer wanted to be married, Isabel withdrew into her new little condo (derived from the word '*condemned*,' she explained), rarely going out. Typically she would awaken at four o'clock in the morning and, unable to get back to sleep, would stare at the ceiling and brood about what she called "wasted years, wasted love." She lost twenty-five pounds without consciously dieting ("that's the one good thing I can say for divorce"), rarely bothered with make-up, and toyed with the idea of suicide. Then, to her great good fortune, two of her wisdom teeth impacted.

"I'd been going to Max ever since Dr. Cornell, our first dentist, died—about four years. Max immediately impressed me as being a caring, competent dentist. That was all. He was my *dentist*, not a man—a very young dentist. Besides, I didn't think of men as *men* then. I mean, I was a married woman. Anyway, what kind of communication, not to mention a relationship, can you have with a man with his hands in your mouth?''

Isabel had to spend an uncommon amount of time with her dentist the next few weeks, not all of it hand to mouth. She and Max got to talking, first about the latest developments in enamel prosthesis, soon thereafter about the growing number of well-known couples where the woman was older than the man. Then, just after Max had removed the second of Isabel's wisdoms, he told her that she was the most stunning woman he had ever met, that he wanted her, and that he had been thinking about her mouth for quite a long time.

"If you think it's hard to speak when your jaw is clamped open, try it when a very attractive man ten years your junior tells you that he adores you and would like the earliest possible opportunity to prove it.''

She fled his office without a word. "I literally ran out of there. I was utterly nonplused. I felt high and anxious. But by the time I got home, the anxiety was gone, and all that was left was the high. I called his office and asked if he would like to come over for dinner—now! At three in the afternoon. An early dinner.

"It was the first time in a year I had tried anything more elaborate than sprinkling garlic salt on a Stouffer's chicken pie. Not that it mattered. We were so intent on each other we scarcely ate. I can't remember if I ever felt that way with Irving. I think I did, but it was so long ago . . .''

Isabel spent almost every evening and weekend with Max. She lost ten more pounds, this time deliberately, and spent money on clothing, good clothing, for the first time in her life.

"I wasn't planning to ask Irving to pay for my dental work on top of everything else, especially now that

I had become emotionally involved with our dentist.
But then I figured, what the hell, for twenty-seven
years he had unrestricted access to the most sensuous
mouth in Marin—that's what Max says and he ought
to know—all free of charge. He could bloody well
afford to pay for restoring it to its original, pristine
condition. I had better uses for my money. Besides,
Max is giving him a deal."

The euphoria that had replaced Isabel's depression
was not conducive to reflection. In lieu of soul search-
ing, she savored the flowers, the attention, and the lust,
and she employed Max's affirmation of her intelligence
and sexuality to get her self-esteem back in place.
Though Max was always happy to listen patiently, her
monologues and ruminations about Irving gradually
ceased entirely. She continued on in therapy with me
only because of a vague, persistent sense that all this
was too good to be true, and even if real, too fragile
to endure.

"My images of passion with Irving are rather faded,
but we *were* solid. This thing with Max . . . I don't
know . . . it feels real and yet, I know this sounds
trivial, doctor, but Max never heard of Fred Allen. Or
Nat King Cole. He thought the Battle of the Bulge was
a diet book. He's got Harry Truman bunched up in his
mind with Harding and Coolidge. And he honestly
believed every woman owned a vibrator along with
their stereo and microwave—another of those major
household appliances no woman is without."

"Well, Isabel, relative to the kinds of incompatibil-
ity I regularly see in this office, the differences you
describe are not the sort likely to produce much
anguish."

"They aren't. It's really all kind of amusing. But it
points out how very different we are. We're perhaps

only a half a generation apart in age, yet he feels in many ways like my college-aged son."

A few weeks later, Isabel terminated therapy. She felt contented and youthful and, although uncertain of the direction of her relationship with Max, was pleased with it wherever it might be taking her. She had clarity about its incongruities and was untroubled by them.

Two years later, Isabel sent me an invitation to her wedding, not to Max but to someone whose name was not known to me. I suspect Max received an invitation as well—and would be attending.

Healing relationships are tender, caring, generous strands of intimacy that serve a therapeutic purpose following a long period of deprivation or strife, divorce, death, or emergence from an addictive love affair. Partners-in-healing may have few of the intrinsic qualities necessary for an enduring relationship, but they nevertheless can provide a soothing, indulgent ambience in which to recover form psychic pain. These are surprisingly comfortable relationships, free of expectations to go unmet, unburdened by thumb-worn scripts to inhibit feelings. But once healing is complete, fundamental misfittings or other heretofore ignored or unnoticed problems usually ensure the quiet end of the romance, unless it shifts to a different form. Most often, however, the lover so gifted as partner in a *therapeutic* relationship is not nearly so well suited for another kind. Even in love, there are specialists.

Certainly, this was the experience of Tony, a patient of mine who, three weeks after his wife Marion died, had an affair with his neighbor's wife.

"Rod was out of town as usual. Ruth came over with some cold chicken, wine, a cake, and consolation. We drank the wine and went to bed. That first night lust was no match for my grief and guilt—guilt that this woman in our bed was not my wife, not Marion. She was Rod's wife, goddamn it. But all that changed in a hurry. After that, Ruth was always there for me when I needed just physically to force myself past the pain. At the same time, she was always exquisitely sensitive to when I needed space and distance.''

Clearly, Ruth cared for Tony. They had been close for years. Years earlier she had enjoyed a sexually open marriage with Rod, but lately there had been little sexuality, open or closed, with her husband or anyone else. Ruth, easily responding to his bereavement with loving tenderness, gave to herself by giving to Tony.

For the next two months, Tony and Ruth saw each other as often as they could. Then, when Tony completed his mourning process, Ruth and Tony did something many would find difficult. They went back to being just ''friendly neighbors'' once again.

Doing It Better

The very *raison d'être* of the healing relationship ensures that it is time limited and relatively problem free as it runs its course. A few additional thoughts about it are reserved for the end of the next section.

Transitional Relationships—Moving Forward

Transitional relationships are part and parcel of everyone's growth as we move from adolescence through middle adult life. Although a few individuals fall in love as they approach adulthood and remain enamored of their lover for the rest of their lives, most of us move through a series of shorter relationships, successively leaving one in favor of another that reflects our progressive levels of maturity. Our new partner usually has characteristics of both previous lovers and our ultimate ideal, a sort of *solera* recycling of the old with the new. For instance, someone long drawn to just surface beauty, might advance to *good looks with substance*. Or someone seemingly hooked on abuse might progress to a relationship in which he or she is merely *neglected*—hardly utopian but certainly an improvement. Old conflicts may re-emerge but are resolved more quickly and with less pain. Mistakes may still be made, choices can be less than optimum, but by and large we learn and profit from experience.

Transitional relationships are assertive and grownup—at least, relative to where we were previously. They embrace larger patterns and are sufficiently fluid to provide many more opportunities for trying out new ways of behaving. Partner choice is now far more conscious and insightful. Problems inherent in previous partners are still visible but are coupled with greater insights for working them out ("He kind of reminds me of Joe the way he is so compulsive, but at least he knows how to relax once in a while and he's not nearly so rigid"). Whereas in the *healing* relationship there is preoccupation with the pain of the previous union, most couples in *transition*, though still comparing new partners with the old, now focus intently upon the new ones.

People involved with each other at this level usually sense that they are in transit and as in the healing relationship, tend to sequester their partners from the rest of their lives (work, friends, etc.). When they move apart, their reasons are always much more apparent to them than at any time before. There is far less confusion and chaos, and the futility of trying to work out the problems is clear. Accordingly, when such love has run its course, good-byes are relatively easy.

In short, the transitional relationship is a hybrid

between your old romance and the new. Partners, chosen with greater vision and deliberateness, though possessing familiar characteristics, offer far greater potential for growth.

Almost all early love relationships are in many respects, transitional. A girl may date the same boy, often one almost her exact age, through high school, enjoying a bond based on the sharing of nearly identical peer values. When she enters college or goes off to work, she might fall in love with an older fellow who, though reminding her in some ways of her high school sweetheart, introduces her to love generated by parallel but vastly different experiences and ways of looking at things. She's excited by its newness and even by its alien qualities. But its greatest value is as a bridge to adult kinds of relationships.

Similar bridging processes can also occur later in life. We are rarely equipped to abandon bad relationships for good ones in a single leap, for there were probably powerful reasons for entering into those bad relationships in the first place. It may take time and practice to modify or replace these earlier motivations.

"You'd think," said Elaine, "that after nine years of marriage to an abusive drunk, I'd at least find or be attracted to guys that didn't drink."

"How did it happen that your second husband was also a heavy drinker?" I asked.

"He wasn't. Not at first. He didn't touch a drop . . . when he was with me. I'd have a daiquiri; he'd have a coke. I only gradually realized that after he dropped me off he'd go back and get bombed. But at least it only took me *two* years to end that marriage instead of *nine*. Then I had three Irish boyfriends in a row. I'm not being racist, doctor: I happen to be Irish myself. But when I tell you the boys know how to drink, I know what I'm talking about."

"You didn't marry any of *them?*"

"Nope. Tempted once, but no. I learn slow, but I learn."

"And your present boyfriend . . ."

"That's what I wanted to discuss with you, doctor. He's Irish . . ."

"Is that good or bad?"

"Both. He's charming as hell—you know what *that* does to me—and he drinks . . ."

"Uh huh."

"But he drinks differently from the others. Some nights he has wine with dinner. Or maybe we'll go out and have a few drinks with friends. But I'd say there are more times when he *doesn't* drink than when he *does*. And when he doesn't, it's no big deal. He doesn't have to *let you know* that he's not drinking. Some of those other guys, mean drinkers though they were, I think I preferred drunk to when they were righteously sober."

After a number of false starts, Elaine had found a man exhibiting the qualities that turned her on without the liabilities usually associated with them. Interestingly, during her initial session months back, she told me her father had been a charismatically charming alcoholic; now, after growing through a number of transitional relationships, she had her necessary quota of paternal charm, less the booze.

Ralph's transitional process, involving his last live-in girlfriend, Lori, was a bit more subtle but no less critical to his growth.

"I owe a lot to Lori," he explained. "Until she went to work on me I didn't know—I never dreamed—that I could own my own business, set my own hours, really make money, and just take charge of my life. Until Lori, I didn't even know that you could wear a maroon tie with a blue jacket. I thought they clashed."

"She made you what you are today . . ."

"You're smiling, doctor, but that's just what Lori used to say. And in many ways it's true. Obviously I gave her a lot of good stuff to work with and I loved the hell out of her all the while, but she gave me an awful lot in return."

"But no more . . ."

"We broke up about six months ago. It was mutual. I had finished her training, and I think she finally got tired of playing sergeant-major. It's funny, I really admire Lori. Yet the women I'm dating now are not at all like her."

"Not at all?"

"Well, they're certainly competent—very competent. I can't imagine ever going back to the helpless sweet young things I used to date B.L."

"B.L.?"

"Before Lori. But they're satisfied with the way I am. As I am with them. They do their thing and don't require that I do mine in any particular way. Just two equals who live and let live."

Clearly, Ralph and Lori had served an inordinately useful function in each other's lives. Each had changed because of the other. Indeed, it would not have been unreasonable for each to take some credit for some of the rewarding qualities of the other's ensuing love relationships.

The distinguishing characteristic, then, of the transitional relationship is that it reflects growth, often profound growth. It allows a great leap ahead, that clear forward movement toward the close-to-perfect, enduring, perhaps permanent love relationship. It is a romance free of the symptoms and defense mechanisms characterizing validating, avoidance, or fusion relationships, is more alive and personal than those directed toward building structure, is possible only for those who have completed the therapy inherent in healing relationships, and is more purposeful than the ambling explorations of the experimental relationship. People in transitional relationships may not yet have arrived, but they are certainly going someplace.

Doing It Better

In transitional relationships, it is most important that you recognize first that you're in one and, second, that you will not pass through unchanged—the relationship is an essential part of your evolution, and you will doubtless come out very different than you were when you went in. Now is not the time for you and your partner to buy a condominium together or forego contraception.

The utility of this observation is probably clearest with what could be viewed as a special subset of the *generic transitional* relationship—that of healing. People are easily drawn into healing relationships at low points in their lives, and it is this very vulnerability that makes it feel so "right." But eventually the most grievous wounds heal. That young surgeon's presence may seem very compelling indeed when you are bleeding from every pore; but upon regaining your health, you may suddenly find during the course of an intimate Valentine's Day dinner that your "healer's" obsessive preoccupation with surgical knots and anesthesia has lost much of its charm. Don't feel guilty—the doctor may himself be growing restless with your disinclination to continue in your initial co-starring role as patient.

Synergistic Relationships—Having It All

"I often wonder what would have happened," said Amy, "if I had met Alex ten years later. But certainly at eighteen, I was just too young. We were both too young. It was a blessing it turned out he couldn't have kids, although I didn't think so at the time."

Amy divorced Alex after a five-year marriage. With parental help, she then worked her way through college and medical school. Now, at thirty-five, she has a successful pediatric practice. During most of this time she dated very little.

"I really didn't have much time for social life. Grades were always important to me, and while I'm no dummy, I did have to study, especially in med school. And I didn't like the idea of still being financially dependent on my folks, so I was never without at least a part-time job."

"Then, after I was done with my training, dating (I hate that word—it's so sophomoric), being involved with a man, seemed unimportant to me. What *was* important was my practice, and even more, setting up this clinic for single mothers. Even if I wasn't working twenty-five hours a day, eight days a week, I wouldn't have been interested in going out. I have always been surrounded by men, 'eligible men,' but none of that stuff had anything to do with me. It was like I just wasn't ready. I had my clinic, my windsurfing and skiing, and I guess I had a lot of growing up to do."

Then, a few years ago, something inside her changed.

"No, it wasn't that biological clock ticking—at least, not insofar as children are concerned. I have plenty of children in my practice. I fantasize a little about a couple of my own but that's not realistic. To do it properly I'd have to take a lot of time out, and you never really get back to the cutting edge of medicine once you do that. But I was suddenly ready to be a woman to the right man. Can you believe this? After years of being quite content alone, I'm ready to get married! I know who I am and what I want.''

What she wanted was a man who had also done his growing up and could be relaxed about his *own* power and accomplishments—and with *hers*.

''The funny thing is, once I became clear about all this in my mind, men—*these* kinds of men—started leaping into my life with both feet. I'd been vaguely aware of the horrific demographics—that a woman my age has about as much chance for a date with a decent man, no less marriage, as being offered a joint by Nancy Reagan. But what happened to me was . . . well, I guess when I got my mind made up, or should I say, got my head on right, men found this beacon leading straight to me.''

Of these men, Edgar, the man she ultimately invited to stay in her life, was also a physician—a thirty-four-year-old pediatric radiologist. He, too, had been married before, to a nurse he had met during his internship. His seven-year marriage had ended amicably three years earlier in a shared custody arrangement for the couple's son. Over the past year, he and Amy worked together, became good friends, then lovers. As he put it:

''After a fairly unsatisfying seven-year marriage followed by three years of bachelorhood, I had pretty much learned what I *didn't* want. Then Amy came along. I can't say it was love at first sight, thank God. In fact, it wasn't until about a year passed that I realized how gorgeous this woman I first thought fairly plain really was.

''I'm attracted to powerful women. I didn't fully appreciate this until I fell in love with Amy, but looking back, women who were my equals or who even put me in the shade in some way always seemed to hold my interest the longest. I not only love Amy, I adore—

hell—I am a little in awe of her. She's truly extraordinary.''

Synergistic relationships are created by two people who have substantially completed much of their personal growth, often after having experienced and worked through one or more of the other kinds of relationships described in these pages. Change and enrichment certainly continue, but this growth is of the sort enjoyed by individuals who are already whole people, who have consciously and deliberately chosen mates out of the fullness of their wisdom and on the basis of mature and accurate estimates of their own worth, place in life, and self-esteem.

Rather than two fragments coming together, mature relationships are made up of partners each with a separate and individual completeness. Their relationship supports continued individual growth, even if periodically the partners must sacrifice being together. However tight their connection, room remains for each to "do his own thing."

Mate selection is achieved with maximum conscious insight about the partner's internal processes. Partners may be quite different or very much alike. If different, their affinity is not based on a need to remedy individual deficiencies and if alike, the bonding is not a symbiotic, defensive melding to someone familiar and utterly nonthreatening. Rather, choices are made according to objective and rational, as opposed to subterranean and neurotic, needs. Surface traits that might be the controlling determinant of choice by less mature individuals are here serendipitous and subordinate to the healthy and enduring qualities. ("Sure it's nice George is rich, but it doesn't matter. I fell in love with him when he was poor, and if he's ever poor again, I'll go on loving him.")

Such individuals, the most mature emotionally, not

surprisingly tend to be the oldest chronologically—usually over the age of thirty-five. By this time, they have developed substantial tolerance, including that for ambiguity. Neither partner is locked into traditional roles—she may do the driving, he, the cooking. Most conflicts are quickly settled (rather than go underground, only to emerge later in disguised form, perpetually nonresolvable). Arguments (and even the most contented couples can have ferocious arguments) are based on real need and preferences rather than on preconceived concepts or ideals.

Synergistic partners are infrequent visitors to psychiatrists. They have come together not for reasons of escape or validation, not out of a need for completion, healing or fulfillment of a script, not out of loneliness, but because it truly fits for their inner selves. Their connections in intimacy tend to be of the greatest duration. The synergistic relationship is built to last.

Doing It Better

Synergistic partners must guard against either of two extremes: on the one hand, ossification into a structure-building relationship or, on the other, a centrifugal spinning away as each partner determinedly "does his own thing."

A principal difference between the structure-building relationship and the synergistic one is the delightful unpredictability of the latter, formed as it is by two individuals both deeply connected and yet moving independently of each other. Each partner can function alone, however rewarding they find doing things together. Each is in the relationship on his or her own terms, certainly considerate of their partners but not having to answer to them. (By contrast, structure builders tend always to do things together, compromising individuation to the point where they cut into themselves.) Synergistic partners can develop fairly complete immunity to the deadening aspects of the structure-building relationship simply by maintaining their separateness and independence and by cherishing the disconcerting surprises that result.

The other chief danger to a synergistic relationship— that protracted periods of separation and independence may lead to a loss of central linkage—is best met by systematically setting time aside to share and catch up with each other and to "exercise" that special connection.

The hallmark of the synergistic relationship is both partners' recognition that (1) *This* is it—a relationship worthy of permanence and of the commitment and devotion that will make it endure (sometimes even for people who live thousands of miles apart); and (2) What you see is what you've got—neither of you is going to change very much. Of course, there will be some burnishing and polishing over the years, giving both you and your relationship a deep, radiant glow, but there will be very little structural change. If that's O.K. with both of you, you're probably set for life.

In short, you do not enter into a synergistic relationship with any expectation that this wonderful love will transform either of you, because it won't. If, in fact, this romance is an authentic synergistic relationship, that transformation has already occurred. Mature love doesn't help you grow up. It's your reward for having done so. Congratulations.

Summary

In this first chapter, we have attempted to define and explore the most frequently occurring patterns into which love falls—*validating*, *structure-building*, *exper-*

*imental, healing, transitional, and synergistic relation-
ships*—as well as two less common, *fusion* and
avoidance. Most of us will probably experience several
of these modes of intimately relating during the course
of our emotional growth, each a way station as we
journey toward our ultimate romantic goals and levels
of personal maturity.

Travel along this road tends to be in fits and starts—
we may move quite briskly for a time, slow to a crawl,
and then zip along again. (To get a better sense of your
own evolution, keeping these eight patterns in mind,
think about the structure and dynamics of your earliest
love relationships and compare them to your most
recent experience. Or, if you have been in one relationship for many years, compare its complexion and
shape now to what it was years ago.)

It is possible to get thoroughly "stuck" at a particular level and seemingly experience no forward movement whatever. Indeed, you might stay with the same
person (or same type of person) month after month,
year after year, connecting in much the same way
(however unhappily) for want of an effective means to
break out of an old, ingrained pattern. You may, in
fact, repeatedly select those who reinforce or maintain
those bonds with which you are most familiar. People
drawn to *fusion* and *avoidance* relationships seem to
have a particularly difficult time forging new, gratifying, and enduring romantic connections. I will have
more to say about such problems later. Yet change,
even radical change, always remains possible for all of
us.

Let us now replace our wide-angle lens with a
close-up one and examine the separate components of
all romantic relationships, for only by modifying and
rearranging its individual parts can you redraw love's
patterns.

III

Components of Romance: How We Make Our Choices, Why Some Work and Why Some Don't

We have seen how the structures of romantic bonds vary dramatically with our personalities and wants. There are certain fundamental elements, however, a few basic ingredients, that are common to almost *all* intimate connections and that determine their complexion, intensity, duration, and desirability. Recognition of these components and how they operate within your own romantic relationships can bestow much understanding and control to your love life and choice of partner, in return for some loss of mystery.

Fit

A romantic relationship of substance and duration is most likely to occur between lovers who connect at many levels, who enjoy a commonality of needs, interests, values, goals, expectations, stimuli, and of course, of fundamentals such as language and educational level. All these elements serve to create texture and bind people together. (Many of these components are age related, which may explain why romances that attempt to bridge two generations are often difficult to sustain.) How many such elements a couple shares, together with how well their psyches fit, constitute the most obvious and reliable determinants of how workable their relationship will be and how long it is likely to last.

Annabel was among many who paradoxically think themselves almost alone in their fear that they'll never match up with anyone:

"I've always felt I was a little . . . strange. Not weird or antisocial or anything like that, but . . . *different*. Different enough that I'd never find someone who would love *me* once he got to know me, or who was enough like me so that I would be comfortable with him."

Annabel had been car-pooling to work for two and a half years with the same five people. Then, this past Thanksgiving, she and the driver, Jonas, were the only ones that had to go to work on Friday. For the first time they talked at length, directly to each other. They found that, appearances aside, they were two peas in a pod.

"The first thing I learned was that he *hated* easy listening music stations. Now most people can take 'em, or leave 'em. I guess quite a few take 'em but I never before met anyone who hated them. I mean, what's there to hate? Well *I've* always hated them. And so does Jonas. With a passion.

"And he's felt a perpetual chill since moving to this lovely California weather. Just like me. I'm from Illinois, and I've always been colder here. Jonas says he's never had a warm day since he left Minnesota.

"Jonas hates people who enjoy the fun of having a dog but who leave them out in the yard to inflict their barking on everyone else. So do I.

"He hates small talk, which is why he has said maybe three words to me in two and a half years. I'm a woman of few words, myself.

"He's twenty-nine; I'm twenty-nine.

"He *really* enjoys my mother. So do I—most of the time.

"Like me he's turned off by all the car chases in the movies and on T.V., just loves having the woman on top, and always thought he was too strange inside for most people.

"He knows what he wants and can make important decisions quickly. We decided to get married the day after Christmas."

Annabel and Jonas had a certain psychological resonance, a mutuality that made their relationship "right." Their common interests were clear extensions of congruent feelings, a way of looking at and being in the world. It enabled them to decide quickly to unite and is predictive of a lasting union.

But though statistically the most enduring relationships are between people of the same age, generation, and geography, and between those sharing similar cultures and background, it is no myth that opposites also attract. Some people either have "transcended" their backgrounds or possess a powerful idiosyncratic, psychodynamic adhesive holding them to an unlikely lover, overcoming a poor external fit. Choosing lovers is rather more complex than finding a comfortable pair of new shoes.

Romance between emotional antagonists is usually constructed out of rebellious negatives, much as we see in the lovers of *West Side Story* or their progenitors, Romeo and Juliet. Often alienated from their roots and all the more dependent on their partners, they rely heavily upon denial or manifest rejection of deeply held feelings and communal mores.

These compelling "mismatches" serve primarily as short-lived mechanisms through which the partners can work out early psychological problems, clearing the way for an eventual permanent relationship with someone who fits better. Preliminary, brief, antipodean love affairs are thus invaluable as devices by which we finally gratify, exhaust, or otherwise come to terms with immature quests for status, or glamour, with the need to rebel against authority, or with any other such emotional responses that have little to do with who we really are and what we ultimately require for enduring happiness.

Adam, a distinguished, middle-aged man from academia, had just left his wife of many years in favor of an obvious mismatch with Josie.

"I don't think I ever saw my wife naked in the fourteen years we were married," he said. "And sex with her was like masturbation—I might just as well have been there alone. Once Letitia actually graded some exams while we were having . . . rather while *I* was having . . . intercourse."

"Yet," I reminded him, "you stayed with her all that time."

"We got along extremely well in almost every other way. I don't think we ever had an argument. We agreed on everything, including, as it turned out, a sense that there was something missing. As for the less than great sex—I'm embarrassed to say this—I hardly knew the difference until I started sleeping with Josie. I had had occasional sex with . . . perhaps three women . . . before I married Letitia. That was it. Where I grew up, you might get laid if you were at the right place at the right time, but you certainly didn't have *sex*. Possibly a brief exchange of genital secretions. A discharge. And I must say, throughout our marriage, Letitia never denied me my discharge. I could have one every night if I wanted, as long as I was quick about it. I was."

"I take it that things are very different now, and that sex for you and Josie is not a problem."

"Hardly. In fact, since my divorce from Letitia, that's mostly all we do."

"Have sex . . ."

He beamed. "*Have* sex, *eat* sex, *bathe* in sex, *talk* about sex, *reinvent* sex . . ."

"I get the picture. You must be very happy."

"I'm ecstatic. *That's* the problem."

"What's the problem?"

"I'm deliriously happy spending day after day, night after night with a Sybarite who has a five-watt bulb for a brain and vocabulary of maybe two hundred words, few of them utterable in polite company. And she smokes and drinks, and on weekends she takes pills."

"A real sinner."

"I'm a devout . . . I *was* a devout Mormon."

"I still don't see the problem. You don't come across as a man in any great conflict. I discern not one smidgen of spiritual angst."

"She'd like to get married. To me."

"Now I see the problem."

"No, you don't. The *problem* is that I want to marry her as well. I want to possess totally this luscious ding-a-ling, and frankly, I want to belong totally to her. I guess I can't feel this way about a woman, be this physically close to someone, living and relating as a husband and wife relate, and not be married."

"Okay. I'm convinced. You've obviously made up your mind to get married. So why are you here?"

"Because marrying Josie is really dumb."

It wasn't, necessarily. Just impermanent.

Both Adam and Josie grew emotionally and were happy as rutting clams during their three-year marriage that followed. He was at last getting the passionate part of matrimony so necessary to his feeling completely connected; she receiving intense devotion and monogamy from a man who celebrated her many sensuous gifts and who saw and nurtured the lovingness beneath her sometimes crude exterior. When each had learned what they wanted from the other, they parted friends and returned to their own worlds, both carrying something new and of great value to their next relationship.

Upon falling in love, we usually connect with someone who at that particular moment reflects what and where we are, who we are, who we deserve, and that we can tolerate. Our lover is a mirror of our inner selves. That is, irrespective of outward appearances, those we choose as intimates reveal our *own* level of security, self-esteem, wisdom, sexual development, and integrity. They are our personal "picture of Dorian Grey"—a portrait otherwise buried in the attic of our subconscious. (For these reasons, our best friend's spouse or lover may never seem "good enough for him [or her]" in our eyes. He or she embodies hidden parts of our friend that we, out of affectionate devotion, have never seen, but as reflected in the character of our friend's partner, are now all too clearly perceptible.)

If our lover plagues us with excessive demands, it is probably because *we* don't know how to set limits. If he subjects us to unremitting criticism, he is merely affirming *our own* low self-esteem. A very secure person is unlikely to commit to someone rife with doubt. An independent person cannot long abide one who is whining and dependent. An ethical person will soon reject even a scintillating psychopath. Few remain intimate with individuals whose self-esteem is substantially higher or lower than their own. In sum, the duration of any seemingly adverse relationship ultimately depends upon our acceptance of a significant portion of *ourselves*.

Her friends called him "Black Bart." *His* friends called her "Sybil Sunshine."

Bart and Sybil had been living together for two years

and spent most of their time alone with each other because none of their friends could abide each other's lover.

"It will probably be just the two of us at the wedding," said Sybil. "Our friends won't come. And my parents would cut me off completely."

"Poor little rich girl," sneered Bart. "She'd have to go out and work for a living."

"And *your* parents, Bart?" I asked. "Do they round out this picture of global rejection?"

"They won't be at the wedding either. They're dead. Since I was a kid. But if they were alive, I'm sure they'd hate Sybil too. You'd have to be really weird to love a woman like Sybil—beautiful, smart, and rich."

The first two qualities were conspicuously apparent. "Are you really rich?"

"Filthy," said Sybil. "My friends all say Bart's in it for the money. By the way doctor, send your bill to me. Bart's tight and didn't see any reason to be here in the first place."

The opposition of everyone around them did not shake their feelings for each other—quite the opposite, as one might guess—but it did give them pause. Sybil's lawyer had prepared a prenuptial agreement, had suggested that she and Bart go for prenuptial counseling before tying the knot, and had recommended me.

"Is disparity of wealth an issue, Sybil? I see you were concerned enough about potential problems to get a prenuptial agreement."

"Actually, it was Bart's idea. He thought it might silence some of our critics."

"I make plenty of money," added Bart. "It may not show because I don't throw it around like she does," added Bart.

"He doesn't declare much of it either, but he's always got it."

"How *do* you earn a living?" I asked.

"This way and that," said Bart.

"I see."

By the end of the session, I had learned at least a little about Bart: he had grown up on the street and had hustled in a small way and then in a very big way, in precisely what manner neither he nor Sybil would say. But whatever he did on the side, he also held a regular full-time job as a bartender in one of the city's more elegant hotels. There, at a debutante's ball, he had met Sybil. She had scarcely talked to her date the rest of that entire first night.

I learned that Sybil, for all her advantages, was something of a ne'er-do-well. She had been expelled from Sarah Lawrence—"not for *using* cocaine," she emphasized, but for *giving* it away to classmates. She liked to party with her equally wealthy friends and then to sleep until noon, easy enough for her to do since she had a trust fund in lieu of a job. Her schedule fitted perfectly with Bart's. Because of his night work, he usually didn't arise until the early afternoon either.

But Bart worked seven long days a week. He saved and invested his money and thought drugs "a complete waste." He couldn't see the sense in buying a gram of coke, "which is gone in a minute," when the same amount of money could purchase him another share in IBM.

Thus, as they so often do, appearances deceived. If Sybil's parents could ever have gotten past Bart's punkish appearance to see the man within, they might have found much to admire, perhaps even seeing him as a source of stability for their black-sheep daughter. Certainly his streak of amorality was no wider than hers, and we must assume, for all her family's apparent righteousness, that Sybil had obtained her easygoing conscience from somewhere close to home.

Neither Bart nor Sybil's friends knew either of them very well for, in fact, in spite of having started from seemingly quite different points of origin, psychologically they had arrived at very much the same place. Whatever anyone might think, they were, indeed, compatible, and fit together well. Mutuality was unmistakable. They'll probably be together a long time.

Need

All of us enter into romantic relationships out of a variety of inherent, near universal needs—for intimacy, partnership, sexual gratification, a family—and, sometimes, as we have seen, out of narrower, less auspicious ones, such as for status, recognition, and validation. In fact, some of those with these latter needs confound "I love you" with "I've got to have you." They also tend to treat their lovers in less than loving ways. Although it seems incongruous to act cruelly toward someone whom you think you genuinely adore, such behavior is not at all inconsistent vis-à-vis someone to whom one has turned largely out of narcissistic hunger, particularly if that lover is then perceived as withholding love.

Need systems tend to operate largely outside of conscious awareness. Nevertheless, when the needs of one partner change substantially, the relationship must either shift to accommodate those differences or wither away.

For example, a traditionally minded woman decides to marry so that she can quit a dead-end job, be sheltered, be appreciated, and have children. Initially, she may be quite content to live docilely in the shadow of the relatively more powerful man she chose to provide for her. At the time of their marriage, her husband may have had reciprocal needs, such as for a family within which he can enjoy near total control (with the prerogative to make the financial and social decision) or for freedom a live-in helpmate provides from little everyday responsibilities, thus enabling him to devote himself entirely to his career.

At first, husband and wife seem uncommonly compatible. Their nexus is threatened, however, when (as so often happens) the woman becomes assertive and begins to challenge the implicit marital contract. Dormant issues, such as her anger over never having choices, long suppressed by neurotic gratifications now surface. With her basic needs met, she may increasingly demand space to explore who she is and to get in touch with her more existential dissatisfactions. Should her relationship with her husband not be sufficiently flexible to embrace these changes, the marriage may break apart as both seek to meet their needs elsewhere.

I have worked with many couples of this description who routinely tore each other up in the privacy of their homes. A few, ever mindful of appearances, then sat peacefully and smiling in my office as if they hadn't the slightest conflict and absolutely no reason to be in marital therapy—but not Al and Alice. At every session, they laid it all out.

Al usually fired the first shot.

"No matter what I do for this woman, she wants something else. I put her through college. We spend summers abroad and winters in Hawaii. She has fulltime, live-in help. Alice, have you any idea how many millions of women would change places with you in a hot second? Hell, most women can't begin to *conceive* of the lifestyle I've provided for you."

"Here it comes, doctor—'think of starving concu-

bines in China.' Al, I've always been grateful to you
for all you've done . . ."

"I don't want gratitude. I don't want a gold star. I
just want you to be content for once."

"I'll be content in graduate school."

"That's six more years! Six more years without a
wife. While she plays scholar."

"You prefer them barefoot and pregnant?" I asked.

"I prefer being married. I prefer having a wife—*this*
wife. That's why I married her. She wanted a B.A. in
biology? She got it. That's hardly keeping her down
on the farm. But it was tough for her to compete with
those twenty-year-olds and raise a kid at the same time,
even with full-time help. So while she was in school,
I had to make an appointment to see her. She always
had a paper due or an exam coming up . . ."

"Of course, Al, you were *always* right there whenever I or Bobbie needed you. All we had to do was
try and get you on the phone . . ."

". . . and now, she wants to go for a master's and
then a Ph.D. in oceanography. That's six years—min-
imum. And then what? Then when am I going to
see you? Swimming around on T.V. with Jacques
Cousteau?"

"Al," I put in, "let me ask you to tackle this question. Suppose Bobbie—that's your son's name?"

"Yeah . . ."

"Suppose Bobbie asked you to put him through ten
to twelve years of school because *he* wanted to be an
oceanographer. Would you object?"

"No. What has that to do with . . . ?"

"Any reservations? For any reason?"

"No. Why would I have reservations?"

"Well what's the difference between that and Alice's
request?"

"Alice is not my son. Alice is my *wife*, goddamn it. And what about what *I* want?"

Alice jumped back in.

"So being your wife means that *I* can never choose what I want out of life?"

"I thought you *did* choose. You chose a wonderful, rich, full life. You chose a life with me. I'm not saying I'm God's gift to women. I'm just asking you to look at all the things you've got, the experiences you've had. When we married, doctor, she was a twenty-six-year-old high school graduate working for a big twelve thousand a year as a travel agent. And she didn't even have a goddamn passport—because she couldn't afford to go anywhere. A travel agent who never traveled."

I looked at Alice but spoke to Al in words I hoped he could hear rather than have to defend against. "I wonder how it happens that the idyllic existence you've generously—and I do mean truly *generously*—provided Alice feels to her more and more like lost opportunities than the unselfish gift it is?"

"That's just her way of looking at things."

"What's her way of looking at things?"

"She never feels she's accomplished anything."

I adopted his earlier position so that he could argue against me (us). "Even with all the things you guys have done since you've been married?"

"I guess . . . I don't know . . . she seems to think that most of that comes from me rather than from her, but . . ."

"It sounds to me like Alice has more need right now for things to be *from* her than *for* her. You can *give* another person just so much. What I am hearing is that however appreciative Alice may be, there are certain things she feels she's got to do for herself."

It seemed pretty clear that Alice's inability to meet

those needs vital to her self-esteem were forcing her further and further from Al. Al's needs on the other hand, were making him increasingly possessive, which only further alienated and repelled his wife.

Yet, paradoxically, great unmet needs can also have just the *opposite* effect upon an intimate relationship, causing two people to almost implode into one another—a hallmark of the *fusion relationship*.

Rick, twenty-one, earnest, powerfully built and strikingly handsome, was not the sort of young man you'd think would have too many problems holding on to the woman of his choice. But he was seeing me, at the insistence of his family physician, because last week he had responded to his fiancée's breaking their engagement by slashing his wrists.

"Rachael is everything to me, doctor. I've never known anyone like her. I can't conceive of life without her."

"Rick, tell me if you can—what is Rachael like? What is there about her that makes her so extraordinary?"

To hear him tell it, not very much—at least not at first. Three years his junior, Rachael was a college freshman, extremely shy, insecure, desolate, somewhat ungainly, but perhaps most important, quite taken by Rick; she had quickly become his devoted student.

"Rachael is such a 'lady.' Quiet, very quiet. A lovely little flower. She was my flower. Almost no sexual experience. Never gotten off with a man. But whenever we were alone, she was so . . . eager. Learned everything I knew in about two weeks—and went on from there."

Within a month they had fallen in love, a love marked by volcanic sexuality, and after just a few months more, they became engaged. It was the first really close relationship for either of them, and in their passion, each nearly consumed the other.

As he spoke of Rachael, Rick's demeanor changed. His face became radiant, his chest expanded, and his now animated body seemed to grow taller before my eyes.

"Something remarkable happened when we were together. It's almost like we started to glow. Wherever we went, people always asked us who we were—were we movie stars or something? They'd wonder about us. Ask questions. Send us drinks. Invite themselves to our table. Rachael was always on my arm. We couldn't stop touching each other. People would think we were on our honeymoon. We were special people. My entire life was different because of Rachael. It was like, for the first time, night ended and I could see daylight."

"Daylight" was an apt word. For most of his twenty-one years, Rick had apparently lived in psychic darkness. It had descended early in childhood. Rick's father, whom the son had striven all his life without success to please, was far more interested in money and status than in his family. His undemonstrative mother passively followed her husband's lead and left her son to fend for himself. As an only child, Rick had been even lonelier than Rachael, who had been brought up in the crowded anonymity of a foster home. In short, Rick and Rachael shared nearly identical psychological processes and, at first, almost swallowed each other up in romantic fervor. Because of the other, each became transformed from *nobody* into *somebody*.

"She had me spellbound. She controlled me. Nothing like this had ever happened to me before. Like I couldn't get out of bed and find my shoes until I talked to her. If she wasn't home when I called, I'd get very anxious. It was scary how much I needed her."

It appeared to Rick—perhaps retrospectively—that

Rachael got some special gratification from his emotional weakness, his growing dependence upon her. When he was feeling insecure, she would become somewhat haughty, but when he felt confident and a bit more independent, she would get clingy and move toward him lovingly again, hooking him back in. Each was a mirror image of the other.

Both Rick and Rachael were alternately euphoric in their sense of oneness and disturbed by what was happening to them. They had a frighteningly intense addiction to each other, a product of their early deprivation. Their common hunger fused them together.

But then, gradually, Rachael seemed to withdraw. Though clearly still invested in Rick, she was having increasing difficulty coping with the idea of a permanent commitment. Finally, she admitted that she was dating another man. That ended their engagement and precipitated Rick's attempt on his life. To lose Rachael was to lose a large part of himself.

All romantic relationships to a greater or lesser extent meet a multiplicity of needs, but when the strength of one's emotional requirements exceeds that of one's sense of self—of one's psychic structure—those needs can take control. The relationship is then imbued with an addictive quality that renders the lovers masochistically dependent. These powerful cravings—common to those who love beyond their means—are a caricature of intimacy. They are epitomized by extreme, soap-opera declarations as, for example, "If you won't stay with me, I'll die," or, "If I can't have you, then no one will."

Emotionally deprived people like Rick and Rachael are particularly prone to such subjugation out of a conviction that this is bound to be their lot. They "love too much" and have inordinate difficulty letting go of each other because having a little is better than nothing at all. They've been convinced since childhood that receiving so much less than they need is the best they will ever do. But enduring love eludes their desperately tight grasp. Although few experiences so uniquely service the human condition as does romance, a relationship based exclusively on meeting survival needs inevitably self-destructs. Like a supercharged, radioactive substance, it is too unstable to last.

To be sure, if one suddenly stumbles upon the "perfect" man or woman, the hardest thing to do is to cool it down a little and simply permit the relationship to evolve. It is all too tempting to force things, predictably with about as much success as forcing the threading of a needle. Even a relationship that will prove to be of the very best sort needs time to form itself, time to allow the partners to find the places where they fit together. The needier one feels, the more vital this pacing and the more important the maintenance or development of parallel ways of meeting one's needs.

So, if you feel you are about to be swallowed up by your own romantic feelings, you must step back and ask yourself: "Which of my needs can this relationship reasonably meet, and which (despite my fondest wishes) can only be met by me—outside of this relationship?" A love relationship that leaves you perpetually starving has little to recommend it; even a potentially nurturing relationship will collapse if it is tested too soon or asked to carry the wrong weight.

Sexuality, Monogamy, and Trust

Sex intensifies and accelerates almost all the psychological processes that make up the romantic relationship. Our deepest needs surface; boundaries dissolve (which is why it is often so difficult to "just be friends" after the romantic phase of your relationship has run its course—the good fences that make good neighbors have been blown down).

Sex brings out our best (we become more appreciative, generous, and attractive) and our worst (we may become possessive and controlling or must be right all the time). Sex so speeds the evolution of romance that erotic union is an excellent way to find out a great deal about someone in a short period of time, provided that one's sexuality is not split off from feelings and behavior. (Men and women with little link between what they do and what they feel are able to have sex with individuals with whom they have no meaningful connection. Their partner's character or personality is largely irrelevant. Such people learn little about their lovers or themselves, however impressive their sexual activity.)

Over the years, clients have described the catalytic effect of sex in different ways. As one woman put it: "I am not and have never been promiscuous. And I'm certainly not about to start now, safe sex or no. But I must confess, I really don't know how I feel about a man until after we've been to bed. And what I learn in the sack has less to do with what kind of lover he is—although clearly I learn a thing or two about that— than about how he feels about himself as a man, what's under the social armor we all wear, hell, whether he's able to take his off at all. I learn whether his head, heart, and genitals are lined up together or operate separately. If they are not together in him, they don't work together for me. And then it's good-bye Charlie."

Said another client: "I learned the hard way not to go away someplace with a woman—not even for a three-day weekend—unless first I've got a serious relationship going with her. I don't care how much I *think* I'm attracted to her. Things happen so fast—once you start sleeping with someone. If it's not right, if you picked the wrong traveling companion, then long about Saturday afternoon things get pretty oppressive. And you still have twenty-four hours to go. Ugh! I don't care how much initial attraction there is, I no longer let myself get boxed into a situation of—how shall I put it—obligatory intimacy.''

Though fraught with hazard, from psychic discomfort and even pain to transmission of devastating disease, sexual encounters have long served as a useful screening device. Going beyond mere physical gratification, assuagement of loneliness, affirmation of attractiveness, or issues of conquest, sexual union is a powerful way for two hidden psyches to connect, allowing the participants to make assessments quickly that would have taken earlier, less "liberated" generations many months. I believe this, more than any other reason, accounts for the inordinate number and success of "body bars." Certainly people can lie with their sexual organs as with other instruments of communication, but it is infinitely more difficult.

On the other hand, a man and woman who no longer feel much passion for each other, despair of its resurrection, yet want to remain a couple "for the sake of the children" or perhaps in the service of psychological and material investments, may try holding things together by turning elsewhere to meet their physical needs. But affairs are usually just palliation. They may help a failing primary relationship persist a while longer, but they also rob the relationship of needed energy. Though in the short term "adultery" can ease symptoms, the patient soon expires.

Monogamy has many virtues to recommend it besides moral and spiritual ones. Primarily, it reserves all of the couple's emotional energy for recycling and for renewing their relationship. (And, of course, it is the only shield against AIDS that is one hundred percent effective.) But monogamy can underpin the enduring romantic relationship only when such exclusivity has evolved naturally and is enforced through an emotional process: not when it is merely an intellectual rule, adhered to by an act of will. That is, to really work, monogamy must occur as an extension of something *within* you, from a decision to behave in a certain way because it *feels* right. It sustains a relationship when it fits the psyches of both partners, and as such it depends as much upon a commitment each makes to him/herself as to the other. When monogamy is simply an artificial, contrived agreement born of needs to control or predict the future, to protect the other's sensibilities, to follow religious dictates, or to adhere to conditions implicit in the matrimonial contract, it is experienced as constricting. And if it is experienced thusly, it is paradoxically, an all too common precursor to infidelity. In other words, if either of you is "not ready" to be monogamous, even a sincere swearing of fidelity is likely to lead to disappointment. Monogamy is a *feeling*—not a *rule*. Monogamy externally imposed chafes and itches, and many people are all too inclined to scratch.

The arrival of children dramatically changes the complexion of romance, enriching it with family dynamics through which all members make further growth. Like sexuality, children often intensify and clarify the dyadic relationship, delineate its strengths, deepen the parents' connection, and stimulate the construction of structure and stability. But children sometimes squeeze much of the romantic passion from a relationship as their price for binding two people together. They can also shake a vulnerable relationship by bringing their parents' weaknesses to the fore, by heightening discrepancies between them, or by intensifying addictive processes. And, of course, a marriage whose success is heavily dependent upon the *absence* of structure—upon the freedom of the partners to live a spacious, experimental, and impulsive life—will be severely tested by the weighty presence of children.

Finally, no intimate relationship can endure without *respect and trust*. Certainly one can be attracted to *parts* of someone and can even experience substantial feelings of love for a partner whose integrity is in doubt. . . . But such relationships are usually devoid of true intimacy and tend to be ephemeral and intermittent. If your relationship always seems to need "lots of work," it may be that the respect and trust necessary for that relationship to last has vanished—or was never there in the first place.

Summary

At this point, you may be starting to close in a bit on answers to at least a few of the questions you have long had about your own romantic processes. Let us look again at some of the questions I raised in this book's first pages in the light of what we have explored thus far:

Why of all the people in the world, did I fall in love with him (her)?

Why do I keep falling in love with people like *that*?

Why do I love the way I do?

Are my love affairs random experiences, or do they fall into a pattern?

Do I send out some signal that attracts one kind of lover and puts off others?

Do people love in the same way each time?

Can love be changed?

The part of the mind or psyche loosely called "the unconscious" or "subconscious" is programmed to respond to reciprocal elements in those to whom we are romantically attracted. Even more than physical features or mannerisms, these critical ways of relating and behaving (and what our subconscious senses they represent) account for the intense chemistry between you and the people with whom you fall in love.

For example, you might have fallen in love with a *cherished part of yourself* that is closely replicated *within the personality of your lover*. Or, you can be drawn to a psychological quality *sizable in your partner* but notable for its veritable *absence from your own make-up*, although you require it for personal completion or maintenance of self-esteem. However constructed, this romantic magnetism can override, at least initially, more objective, conscious, "common sense" criteria for choosing a mate who might be "good for us."

Without doubt, timing also plays a part. There are, I suppose, a reasonably large but finite number of people in the world who possess a sufficient portion of the right psychological combination to lock us in, who will generate feelings of romantic love and who will respond strongly to something within us.

Let us imagine that for several years one of these special people has been riding the bus to work every morning on the same route you do, *but one trip later*. You're supposed to be at work at 8:30 and he at 9:00, and for three years you've been missing each other by thirty minutes. Then, one day you are half an hour late, and suddenly, there you are sitting together on the same bus. Before very long, romantic message is sent, romantic message is received, and you click in.

What if you had met three years earlier? Would the same thing have happened? Quite likely not. One or the other of you might not have been in your receptive or transmissive modes, for any number of reasons (among the commonest, a preoccupation with some other relationship). And *both* of you must have both incoming and outgoing channels open for there to be a reciprocal "take." Or, even given that you were both open to new romantic bonds, the two of you might not have been at the same place in the evolution of your respective romantic processes.

For example, three years ago, you might have been at a difficult time in your life when you sorely needed the unqualified acceptance, emotional support, and adoration that typically characterizes a *healing relationship*. He, on the other hand, may have just ended several intense, inordinately instructive but rootless *experimental relationships*, leading him at last to a cautious, wary search for something solid and enduring—*structure* rather than emotional immediacy. Given this scenario, three years ago you might hardly have given each other a second glance. To make some sense, then, of what's happening (or not happening) on that bus requires an understanding of your individual romantic processes. We are all extraordinarily deferential towards patterning.

The enormous power of these romantic engrams leaves me impatient with the many simplistic monothematic articles and books on attracting a suitable man or woman, on deflecting "wrong" ones, or on just "winning the ideal mate" or conversely, just not loving him "too much." In truth, during those first encounters with a promising candidate, you can be intractably tongue-tied or, heaven forbid, be wearing the wrong perfume or tie. Alternatively, you can be having one of your best days—oozing incredible charm, your wits sharp, the rhythm of your responses impeccable; on successive dates, you might say and do all the "right things." But it doesn't much matter; for though initially affecting the *speed* at which the relationship develops, none of these things is likely to have any great effect on the final outcome. The subconscious is little enticed by good grooming, nor, is it deflected by bad; neither is it long deceived by psychological ploys or social graces. Incisively, your subconscious always knows what it wants, even when what it wants is rough-hewn and unpolished or, perhaps, not even very good for you.

But there is a happier, less nihilistic aspect to all of this. Our romantic processes are a function of where we are in our personal growth—our level of maturity and the insight we've acquired along the way. After we have incorporated what we will from our parents, most of us begin to define ourselves further through our choices of boyfriends or girlfriends—a degree of *validation*. Then there usually comes a plateau wherein we defer rapid individual growth in favor of creating a *structure* for ourselves—perhaps marriage, perhaps a long-term, live-in relationship. Some of us are able to complete our personal development within these matrices, but if the relationships are constructed prematurely and of particularly rigid materials, we may find ourselves breaking out and entering into a variety of other love relationships—*experimental*, *transitional*, *healing*—better reflective of where we are at that time as individuals. Throughout, we try various ways of *fitting together* with our partners, test different forms of *mutuality*, *sensuality*, and *trust*, and explore ways of discovering just what it is we actually *need* from our love relationships and how best to have those needs met.

With sufficient opportunities, there is, for most, a progression toward more nurturing and enduring intimacies. We learn from each experience, with even "bad" relationships often providing eminently serviceable routes to good ones—a way of working through fundamental issues, of cleansing ourselves of destructive processes.

There have been experimental studies of young children who are allowed to do all the choosing of what they are going to eat, day in, day out, three or more meals a day over an entire month's time. Parental guidance is expressly precluded; the children can have whatever they want. Not surprisingly, the first few days the kids hit the candy and ice cream hard, but by the end of the first week, all are choosing relatively balanced diets—plenty of meat, potatoes, and green vegetables.

Admittedly, I'm overreaching when I analogize from this study to choosing lovers. For one thing, few of us can have "whatever we want," and for another, what might be perfectly "balanced" for you may prove precariously unstable for me. But in our search for optimum food for the soul, there is for all of us an automatic learning curve, a built-in corrective mechanism that, if attended to over time, leaves most of us in a better place than where we started.

Now we come to the hardest part. Although it is said often enough to be a cliché, it happens to be true that enlightenment and contentment are rarely achieved through someone providing "the right *answers*." Such answers are "correct" only in the abstract, and universal generalizations, however accurate, don't seem to be much help in modifying our individual processes, or our behavior. Such changes come about only if we struggle for a time with the right *questions*.

So permit me to suggest a strategic self-enquiry that may be useful at this point. Ask yourself:

Which of the patterns of romance outlined earlier feel most familiar to me?

Am I consistently attracted to a certain psychological type of man or woman? (We are not talking about looks or age, but about a style of relating.)

In that same sense, what "type" am *I*?

What parts of me are most consistently gratified by romance?

Where have I felt cheated?

Can someone else reasonably be expected to provide those things that feel like they are missing, or ultimately must they come from me?

Looking back, have there been any major changes in who I am (or how I see myself), and has the evolution of my romantic relationships kept pace?

What changes in the pattern of my relationships am I likely to need if I am to be content?

The answers to these questions (or, more accurately, the insights and changes they may provoke) won't just spring up all at once. Fundamental psychological processes can't be forced or rushed. So try to renew this enquiry periodically, during and after reading the remainder of this book.

The succeeding chapters are devoted to sharpening your perceptiveness, identifying common problem areas, bringing insights a bit sooner, and perhaps accelerating the correspondence of what you want, need, and ultimately receive. Though passion and reason rarely dance together, we shall try to find music congenial to them both.

IV

Your Love Relationships— And You

Our eight patterns—validation, structure-building, transitional, experimental, healing, fusion, avoidant, and synergistic—are *stereotypes*. In other words, they are relatively simple models that help us identify and diagnose the essential and controlling transactions of our love relationships, thereby lending coherence to confusion. But, being stereotypes, they subordinate nuance to clarity. Though you should see much that applies to you, you won't necessarily find your own personal romantic pattern exhibiting each and every element or "symptom" of an otherwise closely fitting pattern. You might even see yourself in several patterns at different times in your life, or you may favor a pattern that informs some, but not all, of your relationships. Each pattern, in fact, embraces a spectrum of severity—people vary in their degree of psychological rigidity and in their talent for finding just the right partner to participate with them.

If *none* of these patterns seem to apply to you, be at least a little suspicious that one of them really does but that you're not entirely ready to know about it yet. You might consider whether: (1) you quickly skipped over the pertinent section; (2) you became defensive and busily explained why this description couldn't *pos-*

sibly be relevant; or (3) reading that section made you feel exceptionally uncomfortable.

Whatever the principal complexion of your current and past romantic unions, and whatever their shortcomings or the degree of pain generated, without doubt they have met vital, reciprocal needs. If they didn't, it's unlikely you and your partner would have been attracted to each other, no less stayed together, for any length of time. Love is never a waste. There is some virtue in any romantic union, even if destined to end and though having brought dissatisfaction and discontent along the way.

But many times we fall into a love relationship that seems to meet but the narrowest of needs, and at great cost. Or, though at first there was a comfortable equilibrium between the two of you, now one or the other is changing so that what once fit so well has become misshapen, constrictive, and nonsupportive. These dysfunctional relationships compel certain questions:

Should my partner and I attempt to salvage the situation, try to change it to something better, or, although love undoubtedly persists, should we end the relationship as best we can and move on?

If our *raison d'être*—say the process of healing (or of experimenting, or structure building, etc.)—is completed, can we both now change enough and in the same way that we can forge a new bond and so remain together?

Or have we passed the point of repair, so that staying in the relationship can only cause us damage, that investing more of ourselves in a failing operation can only bring more loss?

What are the warning signs that a relationship has begun an irrevocable decline, possibly even becoming destructive?

Even if it feels good now, are we deluding ourselves about permanence?

Is it really a synergistic relationship at last, or merely one whose dysfunctional elements for the moment remain slyly hidden?

It seems we do truly love each other—if our relationship is nonetheless dysfunctional, how can we make it work again, assuming that we should even try?

And, if it is all over, how can I best program myself for a better relationship the next time? How do I break the pattern?

The Time to Make Changes

Although just about every romantic union will fit into one of the eight basic patterns detailed previously, in real life, variations within the patterns are almost infinite—in degree, overlap, combinations, and so on. I never cease to be astonished at how many relationships "work," often for very long periods when in my view they are highly unlikely, unstable, and "flawed." Indeed, almost every love relationship "feels good" for a time. Romance generates a natural psychological opiate that insulates lovers from the slings and arrows of reality. Only when the relationship becomes seriously dysfunctional does it start to pinch.

Whatever your particular relationship pattern, there are three near-universal *warning signs* that real trouble has arrived, that the relationship—by which I really mean *you*—must change:

1. You find that you must invest more and more of yourself to maintain the intimate connection with your partner for ever smaller returns, less and less

satisfaction, fewer comforts and joys. And only one of you is doing most of the "work."

2. One or both of you are feeling real pain (not just the benign sort that enlightens, animates change, or heralds a leap forward, and then, its purpose served, rapidly eases). Almost every exchange seems to cause gratuitous injury, and little either of you says or does brings relief. Some hurt is always present, often punctuated by acute exacerbations.

3. You have the feeling that you've seen this movie before (perhaps many times before), and you know, in your heart of hearts, that its oft-repeated script holds no surprises, offers no solace, promises no happy endings. You're getting older but no wiser, and certainly no happier.

If any of these three elements is much in evidence, you will want to put other aspects of your life on hold and, with your partner, look closely at your relationship. In the ensuing pages, I will lay out an approach designed to change what is no longer working while enhancing those things that do. The plan I am about to suggest admittedly will not resurrect a moribund relationship, but if there is a strong, underlying love bond between you and your partner, this relatively simple program can often make a profound difference. On the other hand, if, after exploring the guidelines and suggestions that follow, you only discover that meaningful change is simply not possible, at least you will emerge from this ten-step, therapeutic process with a clear understanding of *why* your current relationship must end and *how* to do things differently next time. You will thus be setting the stage for the most difficult task of all—*breaking the pattern*.

Evolution—Having It Different

Here are ten chronological steps you and your partner can use to gain useful insights into the workings of your relationship, whatever its pattern, to make a good relationship better, and to refurbish a romance that has become unsatisfying.

1. First, stack the decks. You can begin with a quantum leap if you can *arrange situations* on a regular basis during which positive change is most likely to take place. Begin scheduling several "talking about us" meetings each week in pleasant places—a Sunday morning breakfast, a Saturday afternoon walk in the park, a Wednesday evening joint bath. Don't wait until there's an argument or for the exhausted end of a long day to work on your relationship.

2. Keep discussions open-ended, with the focus on achieving a better *process* between you. *Solutions* come later (don't expect instant resolution of problems that have been months or years in the making). Incidentally, try not to turn to friends or relatives at this point—allies who will simply confirm your own convictions and drain energy from the dyadic process between you and your partner. Keep the issues between just the two of you (or between the two of you and a *neutral*, third party such as a trained counselor).

3. The best—and an easy—place to start a dialogue is with an expression of all the wonderful experiences you've shared, a review of the good things that have happened between you recently, and a recitation of your partner's sterling qualities. (All these tend to be forgotten during those interminable fights about what's not working.) Initial, explicit affirmation of what's right builds positive bonds and creates the goodwill and nondefensiveness necessary to explore the parts that are

not so terrific. It also eases the later expression of (and hearing about) pain and anger.

4. *Share your hopes*—what each of you wanted from the relationship at its *inception* and from your time together *now*. Can you discern a *blueprint* in there? See if you can identify a pattern as you explore what brought and now holds you together—what you do for each other. Ask yourselves:

Is there egalitarian sharing, or do you rely heavily on him/her to feel good about (validation) yourself?

Do you have an underlying sense of this relationship as a way station, with where you've been and where you're going both equally visible (transitional)?

Are you using your new partner primarily as a vehicle to experience something very, very different (experimental) or largely to help you mend following an emotionally traumatic event (healing)?

Do you (and/or your partner) cling to the other jealously, obsessively, so that you "can't imagine being without each other," but with one or the other of you excessively controlling (fusion)?

Or, quite the opposite, are you staying in the relationship because it is emotionally isolating and nondemanding (avoidance)?

Is this time really, finally, different—gratifying intellectually, emotionally, sexually, culturally? Is there closeness without oppression, separateness without alienation and loneliness? Do you have the sense of an arduous trip now at last completed—the perception that although issues remain that warrant exploration, you and your partner are truly grown up? (A *yes* to these last questions provides an almost diagnostic certainty of a *synergistic* relationship.)

5. Did you both *expect the same thing* from this relationship? Though unwritten expectations have the force of a *contract*, the breaching of which is certain to bring profound disappointment and anger. Learn its terms and you will not only pin down the primary source of discontent but will make explicit the areas where change must take place.

6. Take special care not to talk in terms of your partner's shortcomings or transgressions; instead, favor simple, personal expressions about how his or her conduct makes *you feel*. Thus "*You're* so close-mouthed" can become "*I* feel shut out." "*You're* a spendthrift" is expressed as "*I* feel really anxious without a several thousand dollar safety net in our bank account." Criticizing your partner only creates defensive loss of hearing. By contrast, first-person expressions of feeling allows your partner to take in the effect of his/her conduct upon your happiness.

7. Having expressed *your* disquieting feelings and unmet needs, *listen* for and acknowledge those of your partner: "O.K., I hear you. You're telling me it's distressing to you when I'm real close-mouthed and there's no way you can know what's going on with me, right? I can see now how it would bother you—you sense that I'm really upset while you don't get a clue as to why. But the thing is, the more I'm upset, the more I tend to clam up. That's the way I've always been, I guess. I didn't mean to shut you out." Or: "Yes, I can see where our just barely paying the bills each month is more excitement than you feel you need right now. I suppose I've always operated on the philosophy that when you really need the money, it'll be there, but I can see where that sort of blind faith might not work for everybody."

Often just being heard and understood will reduce the painful urgency behind the words and feelings.

8. Now that you're starting to have a pretty good grasp of what is distressing your partner, think about ways you can be different without cutting into or being untrue to yourself. Perhaps she needs you to speak your thoughts aloud—especially the ones that trouble you. Perhaps he/she wants the right to some inviolate personal space or expects a certain kind of recognition or acknowledgment from you. Is your partner really asking for that much? (The answer to this question, in effect, also answers the next—Is *this* the relationship we both want, or are we in fact devoted to the idea of something very different?)

9. Finally, if it appears eminently possible that you both can get your needs met within the framework of your current relationship, practice giving your partner what he/she wants, while being quick to support and reinforce any changes he/she makes on your behalf. For example: "I could tell it was hard for you talk about that. Thank you. It helped a lot." Or: "I really appreciate your saving up the money first rather than using the credit card. I know you had to wait three months doing it that way, but it made for a much more relaxed three months for me."

10. And every once in a while, lavish attention on your partner unexpectedly—not for some change in his/her behavior, but just because of *who* he/she is.

Revolution—Breaking the Pattern

The one consistent common denominator in all of your relationships has been *you*. So if your romances are unhappily the same again and again, if all your partners seem, or soon become, very much alike, you're most likely imposing *your* pattern upon them, either in the initial selection process or by subtly but relentlessly working them over once intimacy ensues.

What you may have seen as *choices* were, in fact, largely *reactions* based on long-held attitudes and fears. For example, if you repeatedly "choose" lovers ultimately not worthy of you, perhaps low self-esteem, created by early inimical experiences, is causing you to feel anxious and vulnerable with someone you look up to. You therefore "choose" a far lesser partner, one with whom you can at least be comfortable, even though you will ultimately be disappointed.

If you find yourself concluding that "*all* men fear commitment" or "*all* women are controlling," you are most likely subconsciously to be choosing partners consistent with your deeply etched convictions—or you are quickly getting them to adapt.

A repeated experience of unrequited love suggests that you are choosing fantasy relationships rather than risking real ones. You are falling in love with an image, focusing on your hopes for what this relationship *might* bring. You are pouring your energies into an inaccessible fantasy rather than devoting yourself to a rough and tumble relationship with a real person.

These "bad relationships" are simply the visible manifestations of dysfunctional parts of one's own personal, private patterns of relating. As such, "bad relationships" actually bring much *good*, for they drag the long buried inimical processes from childhood—the heavy baggage of fear, vulnerability, and defensiveness repressed in our subconscious—into the light where we can see and understand them and, when we choose, throw them out. As such, "a bad relationship" constitutes *opportunity*—one of our best chances to obtain crucial insights and make fundamental changes in our lives. Love is a tool for personal transformation, the preeminent crucible for change and completion.

As part of this growing up, most of us must go through several "bad relationships," chosen or created for some specific benefits we derive from them. When such a relationship becomes truly dysfunctional, however (when the price of those benefits consistently becomes too high—too much pain for the familiarity, boredom for the comfort, loneliness for the lack of demands, stagnation for the absence of risk, loss of freedom for the structure), then that relationship and your patterning of which it is a part are ripe for dissolution.

Let us now assume that as you read these pages you see yourself clearly, perhaps all too clearly, in one of the more inimical patterns and feel that you have long since obtained any mileage from it. The pattern no longer works for you, if indeed it ever did. You've given our ten-step collaboration a good try; it didn't much help. Instead, you've gotten an increasingly strong sense that your characteristic relationships are not susceptible to "improvement." The blueprint just doesn't fit you anymore. *It's time to break the pattern.*

The suggestions that follow assume that if, through a kind of self-sabotage, you have the power to choose or create "bad relationships," you also have the power to *re*create your choices. In other words, to the extent that poor outcomes directly reflect *your* selection process, *you* have the ability to bring about a different, more gratifying result.

Let us look at some of the more troublesome patterns we've been exploring to see what can be done to loosen their hold.

Breaking Free of Validation

If you gravitate toward validation relationships, then you know better than anyone how easy it is to get hooked on "the chase." Only by going after "the hard ones," by achieving the near impossible and winning the heart of that glittering, virtually inaccessible lover, is there enough validation power in the relationship for you to feel good. Unfortunately, after the partner's formidable heart is won and he or she finally embraces your "unworthy" self, the prize ceases to seem so wonderful. The chemistry, their power to validate, is lost. You get "bored" and drop the relationship. Or if, as is likely, he or she too, is a validator, you might well be dropped first, and for the same reason. As Groucho said, "I certainly wouldn't want to join any club that would have me as a member."

Clearly, you're going to have to change direction or you will repeatedly arrive at the same destination. This may be the time to stop seeking what you believe to be "your type." (You probably don't *really* know what your type is, or you would have had a permanent, more synergistic relationship by now.)

Be especially wary of successful, charismatic, physically striking individuals driven by a need for wealth, beauty, or status. They may be exciting partners for a time, but their relentless quest for power, prestige, money, glamour, or glory usually constitutes a neurotic, convoluted attempt to secure love by one who despairs of ever acquiring it through direct, orthodox means (certainly not through straightforward, unadorned intimacy with a loving partner). There can never be enough of these convoluted, substitute, meretricious treasures, so nothing you do will ever be sufficient. However well endowed you are, you can only briefly and incompletely stem your partner's hunger. If you are not quite ready to distance yourself entirely from such admittedly seductive but ravenous people, at least start severely limiting your investment in them. Remember, you'll never break even.

Be particularly suspicious of "instant chemistry," less a reliable predictor of permanence than a measure of validation. Go out of your way to be open to someone who is distinctly *not* your type. Risk the unfamiliar, and you may discover a different sort of attraction, one that takes longer to develop, perhaps, but one that may also last.

Try *friendship* first. Try the idea that someone who is quietly, solidly, persistently appreciative is not necessarily blind, deaf, and dumb—you haven't fooled him at all. He may be not only a worthy admirer but an objective one whose perceptions could be incorporated, with profit, into your own self-image.

The lower our self-esteem, the more we depend upon validation to feel good about ourselves, which in turn leads to very distorted notions about what love can and cannot do. Conversely, the higher our self-esteem, the fewer our demands for continuous, concrete evidence from our partners that we count. Give yourself time to be liked and admired just for who you are. This admiration in turn facilitates the final phase in liberating yourself from validation relationships—absorbing that appreciation and making it an integral part of yourself. Once you recognize your own true worth, the seductive power of the validation relationship begins to melt away.

Breaking the Structure-Building Pattern

The persistent appeal of the structure-building relationship is its reassuring sense of place. But the structure builder typically has forgotten how to relate at a *feeling* level. In any event, it's usually been a while since he's taken the risk of trying—and it is risky business. Getting into feelings—his own or his partner's—makes him vulnerable and anxious. It's as if his subconscious were saying: "If I stop for a moment and look underneath the busyness and find that she's unhappy, what does that make *me*? The most likely culprit, that's what. So I'm going to feel inadequate, criticized, responsible. Worse, if she becomes open about her unhappiness, doubtless I'll feel some pressure to take a hard look at my feelings, and that's something I'd rather not know about. Safety first. I'd prefer to just keep busy. Why can't people be satisfied with hard work? Isn't hard work enough?"

'Fraid not. But if you have locked yourself into a structure-building relationship that has ossified around you, you can turn your propensity for hard work to good advantage. Building from that strength, you can start "working hard" at not working so hard. For example, you can work at setting time aside just for each other, independent of any tasks, duties, or problems outside of those arising from feelings between you. This time and place will be just for sharing each other's tender insides. Choose a site far away from the papers on the desk, the kitchen, the yard, the phone, the kids—a place insulated from familiar cues that may trigger a return to your old pattern.

Of course, no matter how far you go, old processes may try to sneak into your luggage; so leave the baggage at home and empty out your pockets. Just bring along a little cash.

Some structure-building couples use up so much of their relationship with family business that there's not much available for just enjoying each other. By way of remedy, explicitly list all the energy-absorbing family tasks and with each ask, Is this job really necessary? You may find that many tasks are performed primarily because "that's the way we've always done things." It's quite possible that many could be done more quickly and efficiently or even dropped entirely with no great consequences. Remember, structure-building is ultimately so deadly because, when the couple finally gets their work done, there's so little energy or time left to spend with each other in active enjoyment. The relationship is increasingly experienced as a responsibility rather than a pleasure.

If planning for "fun time together" seems impossibly contrived, think back to your courtship days and how you both easily managed to arrange your lives in ways that always made time for each other. You had dates. You ate lunch together. You rented bikes. You bought tickets weeks in advance. And by creating definite plans for those dates, each of you conveyed to the other that you were special, important. To despatch a deadening relationship pattern and restore that feeling of specialness, then, return to the kind of planning that was so natural a part of courtship. If you want to be sweethearts again rather than building contractors, you must treat each other sweetly.

Finally, as difficult as it may be for structure builders to create fun time *together*, it's even harder for each to find time just to be *alone*. Whether or not fully conscious of it, structure builders are starved for some personal, separate time, adding to a perception of "the relationship" as a heavy-handed intrusion. So, just like you are setting time aside for activities that are jointly pleasurable, set aside time just to be by *yourself*. Making time for separateness and privacy will let each of you remain distinct individuals as opposed to de facto siblings. Remember that it was this distinctness that had a lot to do with your attraction to each other in the first place, even if a certain sameness then enabled the relationship to work so comfortably. In short, you will enhance your time together by periodically arranging to be apart. Your dully oppressive structure-building relationship will then slip away, and something quite different will emerge.

Breaking the Healing Pattern

If you perpetually go from one healing relationship to another, with *you* always the healer, it is likely that you are taking care of yourself primarily by curing others. All of your energy is going into being a megatherapist rather than into building an enduring egalitarian relationship or into developing more direct forms of gratification. You have become a skillful, class A resource. It should come as no surprise, therefore, that you attract wounded, dependent people, desperate for resuscitation. But using all of your intimate moments together ministering to these partners is bound to leave you feeling empty and exploited.

This is the classic no win situation. Should their wounds be transient, perhaps a result of some recent severe emotional trauma, they'll probably move on to a different kind of relationship with someone else once healing is complete. If, on the other hand, their injuries be congenital, enduring, and characterologic—if this is their principal way of connecting to lovers— then, try as you might, you'll never succeed in giving them a true sense of well-being. They may stick around awhile, but none of your treatments will work because their real desire is not *repair* itself but *attachment* to someone who fixes them all the time.

A new approach would be to practice making your own problems known as well. First, get in touch with what your needs are (it may have been so long since you looked, you've forgotten). Learn to express your unhappiness and wants not as a demand ("I've been waiting a month for you to give your divorce a rest and just sit down and talk to me about us for once!''), but as a *feeling* ("I appreciate how much sorrow your divorce has brought you but it would sure feel good if you could talk with me about *us* for a while").

Expect less, and that's exactly what you'll receive; but if instead you begin to require if not equal time, then at least a place on the program, you will have severely weakened an old, futile pattern and will begin building a more balanced, mutually gratifying relationship.

Breaking the Avoidant Pattern

Avoiders keep their distance because to do otherwise risks being controlled, manipulated, or hurt. To be touched by feelings means to experience sadness and pain—in their own lives and in that of their partner's. They persistently ignore issues, particularly those that might lead to conflict or emotional involvement, hoping that they'll simply go away. Only they don't. And such detachment, besides ensuring the accumulation of ever higher piles of garbage, creates yet another problem: Avoiders have less and less to share with each other and know less and less about what's going on in their own relationship. Invariably they're "surprised" when, "out of the blue," the relationship ends.

Begin a new approach by gradually developing tolerance for emotional exchanges, even mini-confrontations. Take on the little issues first, setting aside a small period of time for mixing it up and having it out, or for what the diplomats call "a frank exchange of views."

Throughout, honor your discomfort and work your way *slowly* toward the more critical issues. Get through a ten-minute experiment in dispute resolution without much loss of blood, and you can probably brave setting the next meeting for fifteen minutes. Doubtless you already manage confrontations at work with less than lethal consequences. The stakes are higher at home, admittedly making conflict more stressful but, at the same time, ultimately more rewarding.

Even marked differences should not be viewed as an inevitable break in and threat to the relationship. Actually, a common aftermath of well-placed strife is further understanding, closeness, and trust.

Conflict is not only inevitable but necessary to vital, growing relationships. Though two people may first connect because of their many *commonalities*, they remain interested in each other over the years because of their *differences*. Granted, sameness allows psyches to meet, but if the partners never experience differentness, they'll find neither passion nor growth. God knows, peace and harmony have their place, but uncertainty, even a little jealousy and anger now and then, can also serve. So let it come out, a bit at a time. No avoidant pattern can long survive two partners determined to speak their minds.

Breaking the Compulsively Experimental Pattern

If you find that you quickly and recurrently lose interest in relationships that at first seemed compellingly novel and intense, you may be depending upon romances for all the joy and excitement in your life, while abdicating any responsibility for their creation. Hooked on novelty and change to maintain a sense of aliveness, you coast along, letting sheer newness carry the day. But once freshness wears off, the relationship becomes dull and lifeless, and you slide into the next romance. Experimenters tend to rely heavily on pleasure while distrusting intimacy. As such, your passion is ephemeral and lacks the ring of truth.

Or, you could be repeatedly vitiating what might

have been perfectly good choices by moving *too rap-idly*, by forcing relationships into preconceived expec-tations and thus short-circuiting the revolutionary process that enables them to blossom and unfold. Immediately exacting promises or focusing too soon on outcomes (in a well-intentioned, countervailing effort to "nail things down") are good ways to leave your partner feeling pressured. In love, commitment is a state of mind, not a written contract. The latter will sometimes follow, but intimacy must develop first and in its own time.

Premature sexuality, particularly, can place a con-spicuously large burden on (rather than be a stimulus to) a new relationship. The disparity between the phys-ical intimacy suddenly experienced and the relatively modest amount of psychological bonding preceding or accompanying it can be quite disconcerting. In such cases, quite soon after a sexual liaison feelings of dis-crepancy arise, an emotional lag that often proves impossible to bridge. Thus, rather than cementing the relationship, easy sex can bring it to an early end. And there's another reason never to accede to either internal or applied pressure for a sexual relationship before you're ready: A partner who drops you for not having sex "*now*" is also the one most likely to drop you *because you did*. As you ought to know by now, experimenters are like that.

Finally, no relationship will hold you very long unless all of you actively participates. That is, it isn't enough to be chosen; it isn't even enough to choose. You must also get involved. Watching a movie of cowboys rounding up calves may be marginally excit-ing, but imagine how much fun it might be were you to get on a horse out on the prairie and join in. So, look for that aspect of your partner's life that holds potential interest and take the time to learn more about it. See if there is a greater variety of things the two of you could do together. Put more of *yourself* in your current relationship, and you may have less need to replace it constantly with new ones that are "more exciting."

Breaking the Fusion Pattern

Most fusion relationships arise from an unreasoned *fear of being alone*. This fear in turn generates a compelling need to *control* the relationship to preclude abandonment. A measure of your susceptibility to this pattern is your willingness to be the indefatigable manager, the gift-giver, in hopes of maintaining the relationship—*no matter what the price*. Of course, your impressively generous "offerings" tend to have strings attached. You use them to try to bind your partner to you, only to end up the one who "gives all but gets nothing in return." Paradoxically, if you didn't feel you had to struggle so hard to maintain the relationship, you could give far more freely and at moments when it felt good rather than giving with teeth clenched, while cutting into yourself.

Start changing the pattern by being more discriminate, more parsimonious. Give only when it *feels* right, out of generosity, not desperation. Love makes a poor bribe. See if you can't discern a drive to control cleverly hidden within your relentless efforts to be helpful. Remember, unless your partner is as hopelessly dependent as you are (an added and admittedly difficult problem), eventually he or she will escape your manipulative efforts to remain in charge by simply saying "goodbye," and leaving you and all your wonderful presents behind. So trust yourself to give less, but then give unconditionally. You'll eventually receive a lot more than when you gave away the store.

Recipients of immense, masochistic largesse first feel guilty and then become resentful of the giver for making them feel that way. Our attitude toward self-sacrificing martyrs has always been ambiguous—history records them with reverence, but their contemporaries were quick to have them stoned, burned, or crucified (perhaps they sensed the psychological stick behind the carrot).

So, in addition to its inordinate cost, your excessively philanthropic impulse *doesn't work* in intimate relationships. Necessary to say, endowing a college library is death to romance. You can buy control for a time, perhaps, but you can never buy love. On the other hand, if you can loosen your obsessive grip on your trusty, well-honed control mechanisms, the fusion pattern will start to come apart.

I am acutely aware of how much easier these words are to write than to act upon. The fusion relationship is perhaps the most tenacious and compelling pattern of all, and the one most difficult to end or even to modify without the aid of a good support system or professional help. By its very nature, it induces you to commit all of your energies to it and it alone, and to concentrate all your emotional eggs in one basket (only then to step on that basket).

So if fusion is the pattern that you must break, try first to line up a few, kind, wise friends and relatives, people who have always cared about you but who, in your romantic obsession, you may have been neglecting. Have alternative resources—a new work project, a special trip—in place to help fill the coming void. And above all, do not hesitate to obtain an experienced, empathetic therapist to guide you through the vast desert that faces you. Even Lawrence of Arabia never attempted to cross the sands alone.

Summary

It is perhaps self-evident that, to achieve more gratifying and healthy love relationships, you must become a person who functions best in love relationships that are healthy and gratifying. "Who you are" determines the kinds of relationships *you* are likely to have. Unless *you* change, your relationships will never be different. And there is no greater gift you can give your partners, no greater contribution to your romantic unions, than to be as healthy and as happy as *you* can possibly be. That's admittedly one tall order, but it is a lot easier to change yourself than to change others. Further, once you change, you alter irrevocably the equilibrium of your relationships, making it far more likely that your partners will follow suit.

Above all, hard as all this is and though often a bleak and lonely struggle, *never despair*. As we grope toward perfection, love is our one infinitely renewable resource. You'll always get another chance.

V

We've Been Having
a Few Problems, Doctor

Generations ago, a man might have said to his daughter: "Mary Jane, we've got lots of fertile land, but little water. Tom's family, on the farm next to ours, has plenty of water, but their soil isn't worth a damn. Now I'm going to ask you to marry Tom so our families can pool their assets."

In times past, this paternal request would seem reasonable. Father ran the show. Life was harsh, and individual aspirations modest. Without books and television to raise more exciting possibilities, Mary Jane and Tom would have probably proceeded to marry. Theirs would have been a simple arrangement—hardly "romantic," but at least one containing few surprises. Each knew exactly why he or she was marrying the other.

Today, however, Mary Jane meets Tom at a singles bar and finds him "a gorgeous hunk!"—strong, tall, reserved, hard-working, somewhat older than she, perhaps a bit authoritarian, not unlike her father (who, struggling to grow crops without water, had little time to coddle his family). She soon falls for Tom and marries him. She explicitly marries for "love"—and so does Tom.

Of course, what Mary Jane is not conscious of is the

extent to which her attraction to Tom is founded upon an unexpressed need to be supported emotionally in ways her parents, particularly her father, were too busy to do. In this physically impressive, staid young man, she sees a chance to get the paternal attention she hungered for as a child.

Now this commonplace scenario, in itself, hardly foretells disaster. In fact, Mary Jane's needs can form the initial basis for an eminently solid, implicit marital contract—provided Tom is indeed a strong nurturing person whose self-esteem is enhanced by how well he takes care of his sweet, somewhat childlike wife.

But here the time-worn plot thickens: For it may be that our Tom's dignified, masculine performance is a self-deceptive facade concealing a lifelong wish that someone take care of ("mother") *him*. If so, most likely Tom keeps these dependent needs hidden, never admitting them even to himself, because wanting to be taken care of is considered "unmanly." He is conscious only of his intense attraction to this delicate little lady who seems so adoring and attentive—at least until, just back from their honeymoon, he makes his first tentative demands and is told—one way or another—"Take care of *you*? I married thinking *you* were going to take care of *me*!"

Mary Jane and Tom thus discover that, instead of the congenial marital contract they thought they had, they have, in fact, a classic example of a seriously *dysfunctional* relationship. Instead of joy and intimacy, it brings disappointment, confusion, and strife. There may be love, but it hurts.

Perhaps it is human nature to take for granted even a matter as vital as our romantic relationships until they develop serious problems, just as many of us do not attend to physical fitness until we start to lose it. As an antidote to this inclination, let us now explicitly address the commonest symptoms of "dysfunctional romance," one by one. I hope this review will serve as a kind of diagnostic road map of inimical elements in your own relationships that, left unrecognized and unchecked, might bring repetitious and unproductive arguments, increasing alienation, and, sometimes, a premature end to even the most loving connection.

One word of caution first: Repairing a relationship in difficulty is harder than most other "do it yourself" projects. What may at first appear to be a single interpersonal problem can prove to be a complex, layered matrix; one issue will often lead to another. Also, as in algebra, fiddling with one side of the equation compels adjustment on the other side. Still, exploring each troubled component individually allows us to frame specific strategies for avoiding, or at least minimizing, most of the major potential pitfalls in your own romantic life. For initial guidance, I've concluded each of the following sections with some suggestions for self-enquiry that should help you deal with, and possibly prevent, the problem discussed.

Miscommunication

Zeke and Ethel, married some sixteen years, had been referred to me by Zeke's internist who had discovered that the taciturn patient and his wife seemed unable to have sexual relations more than perhaps once every three months. Although Zeke was too tightlipped to explain to his doctor just what the problem was, he was unhappy enough with the situation to be considering divorce. Surprisingly, he agreed to collect Ethel and come to me first.

But he didn't; that is, he came, but he didn't speak. Neither did Ethel. Not to me or with each other. So for two sessions I did most of the talking—about "marital relations," the physiology of sex, the various options open to a couple if earlier approaches no longer worked. Both assured me that they "knew all that." They just rarely seemed able to utilize what they knew.

I asked them to tell me what exactly *did* transpire on those few occasions when they did manage to have sex. They told me. I don't think I've ever heard conjugal union described quite so concisely, but it left little doubt that everything was in working order.

"The bottom line, Doc, is that we can do it, but she don't want it."

Ethel showed irritation. "What are you saying? You're the one who ain't never interested."

"I'm *always* interested. And you're always turning me off."

"What exactly does Ethel do, Zeke, to turn you off?"

"She'll shrink away from me. Or turn over. Or kind of close up into a ball. I've been married to Ethel for sixteen years and knew a thing or two before that. I know what 'get lost' means."

"He don't know what he's talking about."

"Would you mind explaining to me, Zeke, just how you approach Ethel when you're feeling romantic?"

"What do you mean 'approach Ethel'?"

"How do you let Ethel know you're interested in making love?"

"The usual way."

"What's the usual way?" I asked.

"What's the usual way?"

"Yes, please. What's usual for you may not be usual for me. How do *you* tell Ethel it's time to make love?"

"I tap her toes."

"What?"

"We're lying in bed, and I tap her toe down there with my foot."

Ethel stirred. "So *that's* what that toe tapping meant. All these years I wondered why you did that!"

Somehow, years ago, playing footsie with a woman became fixed in Zeke's mind as a direct sexual invitation. Perhaps that's exactly what it was with some primordial adolescent girlfriend, but it certainly wasn't to Ethel.

She shook her head. "I thought I was annoying you by being too close. When you tapped me down there, I figured you were telling me you wanted more room."

Sixteen years of marriage and neither had ever addressed the question of sexual invitation. Ethel and Zeke didn't talk about things that mattered. I could only wonder what other unique messages they had sent back and forth these past sixteen years without ever checking out just what they meant.

Partners in dysfunctional relationships often act upon unwarranted assumptions about each other's wishes or feelings and are then hurt when their lover acts contrary to expectations. As with Zeke and Ethel, misapprehensions go uncorrected because:

it rarely occurs to the partners to check them out explicitly;

they lack or are afraid to use the verbal techniques with which to do so;

they are more comfortable altering their perceptions to fit their expectations;

they fail to recognize or correctly interpret crucial nonverbal cues;

or messages they consider universally clear are, in fact, unique and idiosyncratic to themselves.

In short, even people who have been in a relationship for years (certainly long enough to know each other pretty well) can still have the most extraordinary notions of what the other is like because they have learned neither to speak nor to hear.

"Seymour *never* listens to me," said Michelle.

"That's all I do is listen to you," Seymour replied.

"Then why don't you ever seem to hear what I'm saying?"

"I hear you, I hear you—God I hate that phrase—I can play your speeches back to you from memory."

"Then how come nothing ever changes? I'm still last around here—behind your accounts, behind the 49ers, even behind your goddamn dogs. Can you imagine what it's like having to stand in line behind twenty sweaty jocks and two dogs?"

But despite frequent quarrels, Michelle basically enjoyed living with Seymour and the increased opportunities for intimacy it provided. And Seymour was very much attuned to how tremendously Michelle had added to his happiness. He was convinced he missed no occasion to show her his gratitude, *unless Michelle explicitly asked him to do so*.

Seymour had spent much of his childhood struggling to follow (and in adolescence, rebelling against) incessant parental commands. It had left him with a little short-circuit in his brain wherein even the softest requests, the gentlest expression of a wish or feeling, was heard as a *demand*. And demands closed him off. As he put it: "It seems to me as if Michelle is always prepared to forcibly extract a fraction of what she'd get if only she'd let me give it to her voluntarily, as if she prefers a quarter won in battle over a dollar acquired in quiet negotiations. Why must she be like that all the time?"

A good part of the answer rested in Michelle's family of two girls and five boys. As she explained:

"When I was growing up, if you didn't raise your voice, you weren't heard. The squeaky wheel didn't get the grease until it was practically coming off the axle. My parents did what they could, and I know they loved us, but there just wasn't enough of them—or anything else—to go around."

In a word, Seymour's childhood need for armor plating and Michelle's need for Howitzers often shut off all communication between them. The most benign message could get lost in the din of gratuitous battle.

Faulty communication can occur even between the most carefully chosen lovers—particularly in certain psychologically loaded areas—but happily, this difficulty is one of the more accessible and readily remedied problems afflicting romantic partnerships. No relationship otherwise rewarding should ever be jettisoned because of a pattern of garbled or aborted transmission.

Here are some questions you and your partner might profitably ponder to identify blocks to mutual understanding and to improve communication between you.

Strategic Self-Enquiry:

How do I share my feelings with my partner?

Is it true that the more strongly I feel about something, the more expressive I become—or vice versa?

How do I ask for what I want—with a simple, direct request, by talking around the subject or about something else, by making a demand, or by expressing anger about even having to ask?

How do I usually convey disappointment?

How do I know my partner has heard me?

Do I take my clarity for granted?

How do I let my partner know he or she has been heard?

Have I ever asked my partner how I can listen better?

Misperception

"Brenda and I do love each other," Boris asserted with conviction.

"We really do," agreed Brenda.

"If only we didn't fight so much."

"Over what?" I asked.

"Usually over which of us is always starting fights," said Brenda.

"How *do* they start?"

"He starts it."

"She starts it," said Boris simultaneously.

"Not who. *How*?"

"Well, we seem to have four or five days where we're just like lovebirds," said Boris. "We hardly have to talk because we always seem to know what the other is thinking. . . ."

"Our friends can't stand to be around us because we're so dewy-eyed," added Brenda.

"And then Brenda starts her bitching . . ."

"I don't bitch."

". . . like this weekend. First she bitches that I screwed up the carburetor . . ."

"The car stalls more than before . . ."

". . . after I put two entire Sundays into that thing. Then of course it's all my fault we missed the beginning of the movie last night . . ."

"If you'd pick me up on time for once . . ."

"She forgets all about the time she wasted bitching that I forgot our 'anniversary' . . ."

"Well you did!"

"Like hell, I did! We didn't have our first date until New Year's Day and that's not for a whole goddamn week yet."

"We *met* on *Christmas Eve* . . ."

"We both just happened to be at a party on Christmas Eve, along with two hundred other people. We talked for about fifteen minutes. *That's* what you want to celebrate?"

"If we hadn't gone to Jane's Christmas party we never would have met, we wouldn't have gone out, and we wouldn't be together now. You'd think that you'd want to . . . to commemorate an event that changed our lives . . ."

"All right, Brenda. Merry goddamn Christmas. It changed our lives all right. I *used* to have a little peace . . ."

"Mostly what you're used to is not giving a damn."

"Oh, I give a damn, I give a damn all right. But no matter what I do, it's never enough . . ."

"And when I try and talk to him about it, he clams up. It's like talking to a wall . . ."

"You don't *talk*. You *bitch!*"

"When I bring up a problem calmly and quietly, your mind's somewhere else, so then I start . . ."

"My *mind's* somewhere else? Where the hell were *all* of you last week?"

"I told you. I needed some time alone . . ."

"You never returned any of my messages."

"I just needed some quiet time . . ."

"That's such bull, Brenda, and you'd find out how *much* bull if only you'd stop hiding from me . . ."

"Hiding?"

"Yeah, hiding. I still gotta ask for dates two weeks in advance. It's pulling teeth getting you to stay overnight . . ."

"I explained that eighteen times already. I love you, Boris, really I do, but I also need time alone. I'm *not* going to put myself in the position where I have to depend on anyone. I told you that. This way, it doesn't matter so much when you let me down . . ."

"When the hell have I *ever* let you down? I've *always* been there for you. I just don't know what in hell you're talking about."

In work such as mine, one often hears these rambling, circular arguments between two people who seemingly want the same things for themselves and for their partners. Yet, something keeps getting in the way, blocking or distorting their view of one another so that the other appears to be making a point of being difficult, self-centered, inconsiderate, provocative.

Even at the height of battle, one could discern the intensity of Boris' and Brenda's romantic connection. Whenever they felt secure in their feelings for each other, they were capable of an almost supernal, empathetic bond. But when either one felt let down or angry, he or she would level improbable accusations that would leave the partner convinced that he or she must be talking about *somebody else*. And that belief would be right.

The key to Brenda and Boris' unending quarrel laid in the personalities of *two other people* who although invisible, were very much in the room with them—Brenda's father and Boris' mother.

Brenda described her father with great succinctness as "a loving flake." During her childhood, he doted on her whenever they were together. But often he'd disappear or just forget to come home, forget her birthday, her high school graduation, his promise to take her with him on his next trip. By repeatedly "forgetting," he'd unwittingly programmed Brenda's unconscious belief that men inspire your devotion, promise the world, then abandon you. Brenda grew up determined never to let that happen to her again.

Boris' mother years ago had turned to her young son to replace all the things missing from her life after her husband had summarily left. Boris, resonant with her bitter privation, struggled to provide what, of course, he could not. And so yet another child's subconscious mind underwent unwitting parental programming—Boris' mother left him with the unacknowledged but powerful underlying conviction that, although women will insist that you alone can bring them happiness, everything you've got will still not be enough. In time, Boris learned to defend against a perpetual feeling of failure by alternately assuming the role of superman and then seeming not to care.

Brenda, therefore, pulled back as soon as she found herself liking things a little too much (and she was very much captivated by Boris when he was wearing his blue and red cape). For Brenda, gratification meant dependency, and dependency was a set-up for disappointment and desertion. So she'd either hide herself away before it happened, or attack Boris, not for what *he had* done, but for what *her father* hadn't. And Boris responded to Brenda's attacks as would any red-blooded American man—he withdrew into wounded silence thereby confirming Brenda in her certainty that men are never there when you need them most.

Brenda and Boris exemplify how lovers in dysfunctional romances often see and treat each other: as they *expect* him or her to be rather than as that person really is. They miscast their partners in roles better fitting a significant and conflictual person from the past rather than their lover's actual capabilities, and they attribute to their partners many of their own unrecognized attitudes, which in turn, are internalizations of important childhood figures.

Such distortions leave it up to the misperceived partner to resolve the residuals of upheavals in the other's parental home—an impossible task. Because communication is often faulty as well, neither partner normally sees the part astigmatism is playing in the inevitable conflicts.

Here are some pertinent questions to reflect upon if, in Boris' and Brenda's conflict, you heard echoes of your own romantic relationships.

Strategic Self-Enquiry:

Why am I in this relationship?

What do I expect?

What am I not getting?

Have I found myself short of that commodity?

With whom?

Why is deprivation in this area so important to me?

How is its great importance affecting how I treat my partner?

When I'm upset, who does my partner remind me of?

Is my partner *really* like that?

When I'm upset, who do *I* remind me of?

How does my being like that affect how I respond to my partner?

What are the three most important changes my partner would like me to make? (Then request that your partner ask the same question.)

Unmet Dependent Needs

Like Zeke, Lil had also come to me by way of another physician—a neurologist. He had found no physical explanation for excruciating and persistent headaches, no clinical pattern with which he was familiar, no diagnostic clues save one: The headaches had begun a year ago, at about the same time she'd moved in with Jim, her fiancé. So I asked Jim to join Lil in her sessions with me.

He came under protest. "We have a great relationship," he said. "I'm having a real hard time with the idea that our living together is somehow giving Lil headaches. That's just nutty."

"Jim's right, doctor. And he's so busy, I'd hate to waste his time. I'm not so sure even I should be here. I keep thinking that Dr. Avery missed something, that I've got this brain . . ."

-"I don't think so, Lil. You've been worked up twice and thoroughly—neurological examinations, CT-scans, magnetic nuclear resonance—you've been the ultimate recipient of the wonders of modern medicine. Besides, if a brain tumor *had* started to develop a year ago, by now we'd all know about it—for sure—even without all these tests. But I gather, except for the headaches, you're just about symptom free."

"She's healthier than I am, doctor," said Jim.

"I guess I feel O.K. Except for these awful headaches. And I'm tired a lot because I don't sleep very well."

"The headaches keep you awake?" I asked.

"No. I fall asleep fine, which is surprising because waterbeds kind of make me nauseous. But I wake up at three in the morning and just can't seem to get back to sleep again."

"You know, hon," observed Jim, "I don't think you need as much sleep as most people."

"I'd like to believe that 'cause I sure don't get very much. I spend a lot of time watching you sleep."

"You watch *Jim* sleep?"

"What else is there to do at four in the morning? We sleep in Jim's waterbed, and I don't want to wake him by moving. So I lie there hoping I'll fall asleep again."

Jim again looked on the bright side. "I read that just resting quietly is almost as good as sleep for recharging the brain."

"That may work for some people, but it doesn't seem to work for me. I get sleepy at the wrong times. That's how I burned everybody's pork chops last night. I sat down to rest for a minute and fell asleep."

"Who's *everybody*?" I asked.

Jim explained. "I had some business associates over for dinner—except that we had to go out for dinner because Lil burned the chops." He chuckled, "We don't seem to have a lot of luck with dinner parties lately."

"I really screwed that dinner up. It seems like that's all I do lately—screw up at work, screw things up with Jim . . ."

She began to cry. And then Jim did something quite extraordinary. *He just sat there*. He didn't draw closer or put his arms around Lil. He didn't search for his own handkerchief when it was apparent that Lil was without one. He didn't move. Not even his expression changed.

". . . I think I've been depressed for months . . . years maybe . . . I don't know. There's so much to do, and I don't seem to be able to do any of it."

She was wrong there. In fact, Lil held a full-time job in the financial district, kept Jim's house, and entertained his friends and business connections. She made Jim's waterbed and slept in it, even though it made her a little seasick. Despite referring to herself as "the wicked stepmother" to Jim's kids, it was clear that she went all out to make them comfortable with her. She made their lunches, got them off to school. . . . By the time she was no more than half-way through describing a typical day to me, *I* started to feel a little tired and despondent.

Jim, on the other hand, remained undefatigably upbeat. "She's quite a woman, doctor. A gem. You can see why she's my most cherished possession . . ."

"Sort of like—a Maserati."

". . . that didn't come out right. I mean she belongs to me in the *emotional* sense. And I belong to her too, of course."

But apparently not enough. As Lil opened up over the next few weeks—not without a struggle—she was able to shift attention from her own perceived short-comings to her suppressed feelings about her lover. A picture emerged of him as ebullient and confident ("Jim's *always* cheerful doctor—that's what I love about him, that's what attracted me to him in the first place") and *demanding*. He didn't actually *ask* her to do things for him—if he had, she might have been able to say no from time to time—he just *expected* it.

"Sounds like Jim is not totally satisfied with the special services you provide."

"What 'services,' doctor? I don't do anything different than any woman of the house."

"*Are* you the woman of the house?"

"Of course I am."

"So it's your *house*, too."

"Well, it's Jim's *house*. What I mean . . ."

"And Jim's kids . . ."

"Yes . . ."

". . . friends . . ."

"Many are, yes . . ."

". . . waterbed . . . ?"

"Yes, it was originally his bed . . ."

"So what's yours?"

"I don't understand."

"What do *you* get out of all this?"

"We love each other."

"I'm sure you do. I just want to hear a bit more about what Jim gives to you—*your* piece of the love you share. Tell me what part belongs to you, besides the headaches."

Lil sat in silence. Jim could hardly contain himself.

"I'll tell you what's hers. She gets . . ."

Lil interrupted Jim for the first time. "Please, Jim, I think I have to decide for myself what I get out of all this."

Two weeks later Lil decided she wasn't getting all that much. She moved out, taking her clothes and her big iron skillet. She left the depression and headaches behind.

Needy people can fool you. True, some of them present themselves as manifestly passive, dependent, helpless people who can be quite vociferous about their apparent lifelong deprivation. But just as many defend against recognizing their dependent needs either by cleverly manipulating others to take care of them or, surprisingly, by becoming super-caretakers themselves—as long as they're running themselves ragged taking care of everybody else, they've no time to face how little *they're* getting.

The inevitable failure of any romantic union to meet powerful, unmet narcissistic yearnings for an all-absorbing, unconditional love may bring on psychosomatic symptoms, depression, or states of chronic, irrational anger, punctuated by acute episodes of rage. Such may be a woman's response to her lover's efforts to meet his own dependent needs while seemingly ignoring hers; or such reactions can come from a man whose lover's simple presence threatens his independence by augmenting his dependent yearnings to an intolerable degree. Find two people who punch each other out, and you will find a lot of unmet needs.

Alcohol abuse is another common consequence of unmet dependent needs. In a typical relationship involving alcoholism, the man is struggling with inordinate yearnings for nurturance, yearnings kept repressed and unacknowledged because of their potential threat to his masculinity. But such needs are permitted expression during episodes of total alcoholic helplessness, which, in turn, are kept mercifully out of consciousness by the fact of his intoxication. His lover, however, characteristically fights coming to terms with her dependent needs with compensatory aggressive, controlling, domineering, and militantly abstinent behavior. ("I don't need anybody to take care of me. I can handle anything. After all, I'm in charge.") She rarely drinks because she's always on duty. Unfortunately, this reassuring semblance of strength and independence also serves, self-defeatingly, to drive her lover toward further infantilism and to greater alcohol abuse, reducing proportionately his capacity to nurture or provide for her. Convinced by her own childhood experiences that no support or security is to be had from an adult relationship with a man, she offers him scant opportunity to prove otherwise. Instead, she snatches whatever sense she can of mature womanhood by inadvertently acting in a way that keeps her lover a child.

It is reasonable for people to enter into a romantic relationship with the expectation that they will receive far more from this wonderful connection than they could possibly get on their own. The resources of the whole, ordinarily, should be greater than the sum of the parts. But there are those for whom love serves only to enhance a neurotic dependency. They put all their eggs—a lifetime of frustrated wants and longings—in their partner's fragile basket, only to find the bottom falling out.

This might be an appropriate moment to examine the nurturance quotient of your own romantic relationships. Certainly, if you are forever giving, something has to change. But even in the happy but unlikely event that you're always on the receiving end (here the diagnostic clue would be complaints of deprivation from your partner since arguably, nobody ever feels that they get enough), the survival, to say nothing of the quality, of your relationships may nonetheless necessitate some drastic restructuring.

Here are a few questions to initiate that process:

Strategic Self-Enquiry:

Who takes care of me?

Does anybody else help out?

Are they doing a good job?

Is it reasonable of me to expect more?

Do I need more than most people I know?

How come?

Do I ask for less than most people I know?

How come?

What do I do when I don't get enough?

Does that help?

What effect does it have on my partner's ability to give?

How does my partner let me know that I have to give more?

What effect does that have on my willingness to give more of myself?

Is there any relationship between my needs and the type of romantic partners I choose?

Is there any relationship between my generosity and the type of romantic partners I attract?

Threats to Adaptive Defenses

If ever you doubted that everyone falls in love with the person they deserve, you need only to have spent a few minutes with Frank and Frannie, two very different individuals but very evenly matched, particularly in their penchant for battle. They knew to a millimeter where the other's weaknesses laid and had unparalleled skills in breaching all defenses. They attacked with hammer and tongue and knew where to hit so that it hurt. That they had stayed together, although intermittently, for five years seemed remarkable, unless we allow that war itself was their *raison d'être*.

They were already headlong into a fierce argument in my waiting room and continued it without missing a barb as they entered the office:

"When you're going to the doctor's you shouldn't dress like you're heading for the beach," said Frank, his three-piece suit clashing with Frannie's Hawaiian halter and short shorts.

"He's not really a doctor," said Frannie. "He's just a psychiatrist."

"Thanks a lot, Frannie," I said. "Wardrobe aside, where are the two of you today? Sounds like you're back exactly where we were last week."

"Frank's been picking on me again all day."

"I don't pick on you. I just want you to dress your age."

"I *do* dress my age—I'm only a friggin' twenty-nine for Christ's sakes!"

"Twenty-nine—yeah—*not* seventeen. She wears these teeny-bopper outfits, then slaps on enough make-up for the lead in Othello."

"Jesus Christ, Frank. I try to look my best . . ."

Frannie's eyes reddened.

"She spends more money on paint in a week than Van Gogh did in a lifetime."

"Lighten up, will you, Frank?"

"What the hell are you crying about?"

"I try to look pretty, and you keep telling me I'm ugly. I perspire, and it makes my face shiny, so I use a little powder . . ."

"I never said you were ugly."

"Who the hell can meet your standards of perfection? You know, Frank does everything *perfectly*, doctor. Everything is just so. Neat, trim, and controlled. At least I sweat once in a while. Frank doesn't know how to sweat. He has the passion of a bird. Birds don't sweat, do they?"

The tide of battle had turned. Frank's swaggering demeanor faded, and he actually began to shrink down a bit in his chair as Frannie unleashed her counter-offensive.

"Frank eats like a bird, chews each mouthful in his beak thirty-nine times. He makes love like a bird too—a computerized bird. He's programmed to kiss me first—*always* start with a kiss—then suck on each tit thirty-nine seconds, first the right, then the left, then put it carefully inside and give thirty-nine little bird strokes . . ."

Frannie, though a very attractive woman, harbored

substantial doubts about her appearance, indeed, doubts about her value as a woman. Frank unerringly homed in on her largest insecurity while dealing with his own area of fragility through his masterful precision, perfectionism, and control. And Frannie struck back with withering sarcasm, belittling him where she knew him to be the most vulnerable—in the bedroom.

One of the best measures of romantic success is the degree to which the lovers support each other emotionally. Both experience the accomplishments and well-being of the one as a favorable reflection on the other; that is, "The better off *you* are, the better it is for *me*."

By contrast, a hallmark of dysfunctional romance is when lovers seek security at the expense of their partner: that is, "The smaller you get, the bigger I feel." Frank and Frannie tore each other down in order to buoy their own sinking self-esteems. But such attacks, having further *lowered* the self-esteem of the other, only ensured a counterattack, and so on, in a vicious circle.

A *healthy* love relationship provides both partners a large measure of security that is not as readily attainable alone. But *dysfunctional* partners fail to support each other's defenses against anxiety and doubt, either because:

1. self-esteem is so low that each is too intent on seeking relief for himself or herself to notice the anxiety of the other;
2. each is unable to distinguish behavior that might well buttress the other's security system from behavior likely to be perceived as a threat;
3. both harbor deep-rooted notions that help for one partner can only be obtained at the expense of the other (the "finite pie" syndrome—"a larger piece for you means a smaller one for me");

4. the anxiety felt by one partner may be so severe that it causes him or her to distort, misuse, reject, or in other ways render ineffective the help his or her lover might be willing to provide; or

5. both lovers are compelled to obtain security from the knowledge that he or she can *control* the other rather than from the unifying, pleasurable process of reaching mutually satisfying goals through cooperation and sharing skills.

Some years ago, I worked briefly with a couple whose family business was on the verge of bankruptcy. The husband had started the business from scratch, building it up into a fairly large and profitable enterprise. Then disaster struck in the form of a technological breakthrough by an overseas competitor.

As the company began to slip away from him, he became anxious and depressed, which in turn crippled his ability to deal with the financial blows raining down upon him. Early in his marriage, his wife had demonstrated considerable business acumen, but the corporation had been inherently prosperous for so many years that she had long been content to relegate herself to the sidelines. Now, however, seeing her husband and his life's work going under, she rushed in to help.

His response? He pushed her away in anger, experiencing her offer of herself and her wisdom as further evidence that he was a failure. Like a drowning man, he panicked and fought off his rescuer. The business indeed collapsed shortly thereafter, and several months later his wife, unable to contain her resentment, ended their marriage.

There seems no limit to the conflicts that can bring unhappiness to a love affair or marriage, *without* necessarily jeopardizing its stability; in fact, neurotic bonds are at times more tenacious than healthy ones. But a relationship that seriously threatens the individual security systems of its participants is likely to be fragmented and short-lived.

Strategic Self-Enquiry:

Is there a pattern to the things that make me angry?

Do they spring from out of the blue, or does what *I say or do* in some way bring these things into my life?

Do I feel hurt, anxious, small, or put down just before I get mad?

Is there any predictability to my partner's anger?

Do I play any part in that pattern?

What do I need most from my partner, and how do I go about getting it?

What does my partner need most from me, and how does he or she go about getting it?

What makes my partner feel terrific?

What gets in the way of my seeing that my partner gets it?

Have I ever asked my partner if there's something I do that gets in the way of his or her making me feel terrific?

Fear of the Unfamiliar

Every so often, someone discovers that if there's anything worse than not getting what he wants, it's getting it. Don found this out shortly after his wife conceived a child.

"We had been married almost three years. I'm such a straight arrow and homebody. Kitt's little 'habits' triggered lots of fights. Yeah, I knew what she was like going in, and I thought it would be all right 'cause I was so nuts about her. But it wasn't. I tried, but I couldn't stand her friends and the way they'd sit around—in *our* home—smoking pot and talking garbage. What a stupid waste of time for such a brainy woman.

"Another thing we fought about was dancing—*her* dancing. She loved to dance. I've got two left feet, both of them flat. So, liberated fellow that I thought I was, she could go out all night and dance her little legs off. Fine with me. Only the next morning we'd fight 'cause I felt excluded.

"Otherwise, we got along. And when she went out with her pals, she picked up these great stories all the time. So, I guess you could say that we had our differences, even heated differences, but basically our relationship worked. I'd be pissed off for a little while when she'd be involved with her idiot friends or some activities outside our relationship, but I sure loved all the times in between. Kitty is the most interesting woman I've ever met. No one's ever come close. That's why I married her.

"Then she got pregnant. Right away she stopped smoking pot—didn't want our kid to start life stoned. I was real glad about that. Then, when she got big, she stopped dancing. Then she gave up red meat. Shortly after Butchie was born, most of her friends stopped visiting. I guess they had no patience being around a little kid.

"It's been two years now, and Kitt's turned out to be a great mother. She dotes on Butch, spends a lot of time in the house now with him, hardly ever goes anywhere without him. We never fight anymore. I'm bored to tears. It was her birthday last week, and I bought her some marijuana.''

There are those for whom the predictable, however unpleasant, is relatively less discomforting than the unknown, whatever hope it promises for the future. They fear surprises (even potentially happy ones) and unconsciously select lovers with whom they can live out the same unresolved conflicts they knew in their childhood homes. They choose lovers who embody some of the same elements that obstructed resolution of their parents' conflicts. Though eternally harboring the dream that this time the outcome will be different, they continue in the old, familiar, but unproductive pattern, slaves to their upbringing. Should one such relationship collapse, more often than not they'll recreate it with another partner selected according to the same unpromising, subterranean criteria (as with the woman described in an earlier section who married and divorced a succession of alcohol abusers).

How well you can play the required role greatly enhances your partner's ability to project what he or she wishes to see—a square picture fits poorly on a round screen. Indeed, some people tend to select repeatedly and with uncanny accuracy lovers who do, to some extent, conform to, or who can be pressured into conforming to, their concept of what they *should* be like.

For example, a woman chooses a man she *hopes* won't treat her as her father did, but she *expects* from past experiences that he, ''being a man,'' probably will. Often the man does indeed behave exactly like her father, either because she subconsciously picked him for that ability or because she acts to make him conform to her expectations. She's able to continue to live with him, however unhappily, because she was trained as a child to deal with his behavior, perhaps by developing somatic complaints, by acting out, or by withdrawal. In fact, although she may complain about him vociferously, should therapeutic pressure change the homeostasis so that, instead of her dismal *expectations*, the relationship achieves her fondest *hopes*—and not, incidentally, changing from the *known* to the *unfamiliar*—she may become anxiously aware of just how much she secretly prefers things in the old way. So she perpetuates a pattern present in her parental home and now, to a greater or lesser extent, in her own. (If, at first, the pattern was in evidence only to a lesser extent, over-reaction to each other will soon raise it to a greater one.)

Such people might well sabotage their partners' attempts to cure the very symptoms that appear to cause so much dissension between them, lest their elimination clear the field for exposure of their own problems. The man whose wife ceases to be "frigid" might suddenly find himself impotent; the woman whose husband's now relieved social anxieties no longer confine them to the house may for the first time confront her own phobia for public places.

They may see in their partner's attempts at healthy self-assertion a threat to their own autonomy, and they will set up elaborate covert rules that suppress expression of innocent differences. Or they might be intolerant of the inevitable, benign episodes of regression so often prerequisite to subsequent spurts of growth or a change in fixed attitudes; that is, they won't permit things to get a bit worse for a little while as a step toward getting much better. And of course, the partner's entrance into counseling for "his" problems seems like a great idea until change actually begins, upsetting the couple's neurotic equilibrium.

In short, conflicts can sour romance between those who appear to be "good matches" as well as between those who do not. If lovers are very much alike, either can still lash out at qualities in the other that are despised in himself or herself. If unlike, conflict can arise less from the differences themselves than from the threat these pose to self-esteem and established patterns of behavior, or from efforts to force the other into more familiar molds.

The problem plaguing dysfunctional romantic relationships are rarely the mischief of a single culprit. Nor is there very often a single injured party. For example, though a woman's sexual unresponsiveness may be partially to blame for her partner's infidelity, his faithlessness may also be an element of his long standing pattern of flamboyant, poorly controlled sexual impulses, the very qualities that unconsciously drew her to him in the first place, when she sought a remedy for her sexual inhibition.

Romance is a reciprocal system. Both lovers are party to it and can be counted upon to resolutely act out their roles in a fashion mutually (if tacitly) agreed upon.

Doubtless you have already heard that you risk disappointment by marrying or even connecting romantically with someone possessing many objectionable traits, in the expectation that "love will change all that." It won't. At least not very much, and not for very long. If someone quits smoking "for *your* sake," one week later they'll be sneaking cigarettes, two weeks later they'll be back to a pack a day. Love, however romantic, can't turn a poor choice of partner into a good one.

But what a loving relationship *can* do is provide a supportive environment wherein you and your lover can risk making changes, take emotional chances, and try giving up those old defense mechanisms that have long become counterproductive. A successful romance can make the daring and unfamiliar far less frightening. To that extent, yes, love does transform.

Strategic Self-Enquiry:

What's awfully familiar about the way this relationship is going?

Is there something about it I don't like, and if so, have I experienced the same sort of unpleasantness before?

How did I deal with it then?

Did it work?

How am I dealing with it now?

Does that work any better?

Is there some large fringe benefit hidden inside the pain?

What would happen to me if all the pain and unpleasantness went away—what would I do then?

Summary

A time may come in any relationship when even the most diligent self-enquiry is simply not enough. You feel stuck. It's hard to see where to go next. The answers just won't come. This might be a signal that several sessions with a psychotherapist would be profitable.

The psychotherapist's style, school of thought, or academic degree are less important than his or her reputation for empathy. An implicit goal of almost *all* psychotherapies is to assist people to make a success of their love relationships. Should that success not be

possible, counseling should at least help you recognize
the dimensions of your reciprocal systems, understand
why they break down, and discover your own unwitting contribution to that process. Adapting Santayana,
"Those who do not learn from their past are condemned to repeat it."

VI

Effecting Repairs

Several guiding maxims have evolved during the course of my therapeutic work with couples. Reviewing these maxims may help keep things clear between you and your partner, reduce stress, heal old wounds and prevent new ones, untangle crossed wires, improve the quality of your choices, and reduce the price you may be paying for intimacy. In the process, you may also come to be considerably more accepting and appreciative of yourself. This last is an essential step, since a loving relationship with *another* requires that you first have one with *yourself*.

Maxim 1: Neither you nor your partner is likely to understand what's being said unless you're both willing to hear.

Even when the words themselves are clear, their context and the "deafening" feelings they evoke in the listener often make it impossible for the brain to take them in. Fortunately, there are ways to substantially reduce emotional static and improve communication in any romantic relationship.

First, be truly there, with your mouth closed, and *listen*, both to what your partner says and to what he or she means. That kind of listening takes a lot of focused attention, and you can't do it if ninety percent of your brain is busy formulating your next response. Then, to make sure you've got it right and to let your lover know he/she has been heard, give it back: "Let's see, you're telling me that I don't take hints very well." Or: "I hear you saying that even when I'm just joking around I can still hurt your feelings."

Next, when you are upset about something your partner has done, be careful not to put your anger or pain in the form of a criticism that implies negative intent on your lover's part—"*You're* always looking for ways to pass the buck to me." Instead, state your complaint or wish for change in the form of *your feelings* (as opposed to your partner's transgression)—"*I feel* overwhelmed when it's always me who has to deal with all the garbage." That is, instead of suggesting to your lover that he or she is a cowardly shirker, arguably an unwarranted and presumptuous *judgment* (and one guaranteed to shut down all further communication for a week), simply tell him/her how you experience what's going on. Comment less on what *your partner* does, and more on how *you* feel.

So, rather than declaring that, "It's obvious your work is more important than my happiness," you might share that, "I feel alone and abandoned when you work twelve hours straight." Your lover can justly challenge your right to put him/her down, but no one can dispute your right to your own feelings. Expressing these parts of yourself rather than criticizing your lover is far less likely to generate defensiveness.

Similarly, it is often possible to restate or rephrase your partner's accusations against you into statements that will allow constructive forward motion. For example, if he says something awful and dead-end, like "You're really dense today," you might grit your teeth a bit and reply, "No, I'm not at all, but I hear your frustration with me when I don't seem to be in step with you.''

I'll admit that to reword fixed, negative judgments into fluid feelings requires skill, practice, and patience, but there is no better way to open up, lighten, liquefy, and render fruitful an otherwise pointless, hurtful argument. Search for and respond only to the positive elements (however small) in the verbal thunderbolts coming your way, and defenses will dissolve, agitation will fade, voices will grow softer, and people will hear one another.

Maxim 2: Your body may know more about your relationships than you do, so listen to your body and honor what it has to say.

One of my more memorable recent clients was a twenty-year-old woman referred to me by her perplexed dermatologist. He had thrown up his hands after trying every therapeutic trick he knew of to clear up his patient's particularly tenacious rash. Liquid nitrogen, ultraviolet radiation, methotrexate, laser bombardment, steroids—nothing worked. The itching, redness, and swelling continued undiminished. Finally, more out of desperation than because of any faith in the power of psychiatry, he sent her to me.

My new referral was strongly possessed of traditional social attitudes perhaps more familiar to earlier generations. She was convinced that marriage was the only acceptable way of life for a woman—certainly for *this* woman. As she explained, ''I just want a home with a white picket fence, a husband, and no fewer than three children. Since I was a little girl, *that's* really what I wanted.'' And in fact, within the last thirty-six months she had been engaged to be married no fewer than four times.

But she had broken each engagement. Though twice making it as far as the church, she panicked moments before the wedding and called things off. Clearly, here was a woman under considerable stress and in severe, albeit unrecognized, conflict over issues of intimacy and commitment.

And the location of that intractable rash? *It was limited to a small circular band of skin around the fourth finger of her left hand.*

The mind and body are one. So be suspicious if, coincident with initiating your current relationship, you are suddenly plagued by such unpleasantnesses as persistent eczema or headache, insomnia, back pain, or gastrointestinal gas, or if you've become increasingly involved with drugs or alcohol. Chances are you have some grave, unexpressed, even unrecognized misgivings about this particular romantic experience, and possibly a severe allergy to this particular lover. Probably, although this relationship is what you *think* you want (why else would you be there?), in truth you are *not* getting your basic needs met. My advice? Ask yourself a few more questions:

What kind of relationship do I deserve?

What needs must a relationship meet for it to work for me?

Is my current partner equal to the task?

Is it reasonable to expect that he/she can provide these things?

What's getting in the way of my receiving what I need?

Can I get these needs met outside the relationship?

Do I want to?

Is it realistic to expect my lover to change so that he/she can better meet these needs?

Would it not be more realistic either for me to change or for me to change lovers?

Ultimately, it doesn't matter how many redeeming qualities your current lover may possess; if he or she is making you sick, angry, or depressed or just leaves you perpetually hungry and undernourished, it's time to bring the relationship to a halt.

Maxim 3: If you want your life to be different you'll have to do things differently.

That may seem obvious and simple, so let me say it another way. *If you want your life to change, you'll have to change the way you do things.*

A forty-three-year-old, good-looking male professor of literature complained bitterly to me for months of the shallowness of his relationships. The women he saw were all bright enough and apparently quite attractive, but none ever offered the depth or commonality of interest to sustain a romantic connection of more than few months.

"Certainly," he lamented, "I could never marry any of them. And I really want to get married! It's been a long time since I've gotten much pleasure from being single. Men have biological clocks of their own, you know."

And whom did the professor date? Students. Graduate students, undergraduates—their ages ranged all the way up to a doddering twenty-five. Though he was capable of plumbing the profundities of Elizabethan sonnets, with women he went no deeper than their youthful skin.

But he saw nothing amiss. "I'm a teacher. Naturally, most of the women I meet are students. I'm attracted to them, they're flattered by my attention. So that's who I date. It's sort of inevitable."

Yet a constant figure in our weekly therapeutic dialogues, brought up again and again, was a colleague in a related arts and science department, a woman about his age and of whom he was quite clearly fond. Almost daily they had coffee after classes, and they would engage in long conversation whenever they met in the faculty lounge. In nearly every one of our sessions he talked warmly about her, but only as a *person*, not as a *female*. In fact, in contrast to his very visual descriptions of his transient young women, he never volunteered the slightest information about his faculty friend's physical appearance. So one day, I asked him, and he said:

"Lucille? Let's see. How would I describe Lucille? Lucille is . . . well, she's certainly striking. Very striking. Maybe too striking for her own good. Her chairman still doesn't take her seriously."

"You do, though."

"Yes, yes, I do. Of course I do."

"And you find her attractive?"

"I guess you could say that . . ."

"She's 'available'?"

"I suppose."

"And you enjoy her company?"

"Yes . . ."

"So why aren't you guys going out?"

"Going out? She's . . . she's forty-five."

"So?"

"I don't date middle-aged women."

"Like . . . like you don't eat raw fish."

"I don't understand."

"It sounds like a rule you have."

"It's not exactly a rule . . . it's just that there's no shortage of smart, eager, pretty young women around, and I just don't see myself getting involved with an older one."

"Your social environment is no doubt enviable. But I can't help wondering if your age policy isn't what's behind much of your dissatisfaction."

He didn't see it. He was sure that, if he kept hitting on students, sooner or later one would click. As of this writing, he has yet to ask Lucille—or any other age-appropriate woman—out for a date. He's still bouncing from cradle to cradle, bored to tears. And each relationship is shorter than the last.

If you want your life to be different, see if your set of "*I don'ts*" can't be replaced with, "*For a change, I'm going/not going to . . .*" For example:

"For a change, I'm going to take a trip alone."

"For a change, I'm going to take the initiative."

"For a change, I'm going to date someone of a different race or ethnic group from mine."

"For a change, I'm not going to talk about work."

"For a change, when I'm not having fun, I'm going to stop smiling and say so."

These are hardly major changes, but they can be change enough. The point is, it's *your* life. If you want a new one, *you're* the one who's going to have to be different. The new and unfamiliar is often uncomfortable and rather scary: but, I promise, risk a few changes, and the world will respond.

Maxim 4: Past is prologue.

People don't really pick lovers who are "wrong" for them, however painful or ill advised their choice may appear to be. Invariably, there is a good reason for their selection—an emotional process to be completed, a discovery to be made, a psychological problem to be worked through, a tough lesson to be learned. In other words, each of our successive choices of lover has been right for us *at that moment in our lives*, providing the education, comfort, stimulation, recognition, or salvation needed at that particular stage of our development. The more we learn about these past relationship patterns, the more we both illuminate hidden determinants of our decision-making processes and find out who we really are.

I suggest that you make a list of every relationship that's been meaningful in your life, starting with your parents. For each, list three things you learned from or got out of the connection, be they good or bad, right or wrong (e.g., "I learned not to speak my mind"; "I learned never to give up"; "I learned that looks are more important than brains"). Next, write down what that bit of instruction cost you ("I'm still angry about all these things I've got locked inside"; "I never know when to quit"; "I found out a lot about taking care of a smooth, young complexion, but nothing at all about the care and feeding of a middle-aged brain").

Then turn to your current relationship and put it in comparable historical perspective. Ask yourself what you're likely to say about it in ten years ("Well, it sure beat being alone"; "The most fun I've ever had in my life, but I always knew it wouldn't last").

Analyzing your relationships in this fashion and fitting them into your evolutionary path is not just an academic exercise; it is a good way to piece together the mosaic of your life and to start taking charge of what happens to you. You can see what elements worked, what didn't, and the price you paid for each.

You can begin to visualize better alternatives, even if you are not quite ready to adopt them. In short, you can use the joys and the pain of the past to service your future.

VII

Why Love Ends

Remember the princess who kissed the frog
so he became a prince? At first they danced
all weekend, toasted each other in the morning
with coffee, with champagne at night and
always with kisses
Perhaps it was in bed after the first
year had ground around she noticed he had
become cold with her. She had to sleep
with a heating pad and down comforter.
His manner grew increasingly chilly and
damp when she entered a room. He spent
his time in water sports, hydroponics,
working on his insect collection.
Then in the third year when she said to
him one day, "my dearest, are you taking
your vitamins daily, you look quite
green," he leaped away from her.
Finally on their fifth anniversary she
confronted him. "My precious, don't you
love me any more?" He replied, "Rivet. Rivet."
Though courtship turns frogs into princes,
marriage turns them quietly back.

"A Story Wet as Tears"
Marge Piercy

Much has been written about the excitement of falling in love, the joy of being loved in return, and the pain of losing one's lover or, perhaps, never really winning one's lover in the first place. We hear little, however, about *falling out of love*, usually because we don't recognize what's happening until after it's happened. Even more puzzling than falling in love with the "wrong" person are the ways in which we lose our passion for someone we once found worthy of our deepest feelings. Let's try to make some sense out of that experience.

Final Processes

"It happened so suddenly," my new client, still astonished, tried to explain. "One day I loved him; the next day I didn't."

Over the course of Susie's ten-year marriage, she had managed to accept her husband's several brief affairs with some stoicism. "They hurt, hurt terribly, of course. But I loved Raymond deeply, and I kept on loving him. And these three women apparently meant little to him—however much what had happened meant to me. Then, about a week ago, I discovered he'd started with this . . . 'Sunny,' our neighbor. That was it!"

"Now I don't feel hurt. I don't even feel sorrow or loss anymore. Just . . . nothing. Ten years of loving that man and all of a sudden, it's gone. I don't understand. His affair with Sunny was no different than the others . . ."

Susie had reported an experience I had heard described all too often in my psychotherapeutic work with couples in distress. Seemingly, that love is very much like a reservoir, and over time, it can be replenished and enlarged or it can be drawn upon, even drained. People in love rarely sense how close to empty this reservoir of feelings for their partner may be. Except, perhaps for an occasional bit of sediment, the last drops, even the final one, seem little different from the first. Although most of us can vividly recall each step of falling *in* love, the process of falling *out* of love is largely invisible, until completed.

Each time Raymond "cheated," the resulting depletion of Susie's emotional connections with him, though substantial, was imperceptible to her through her pain. Her initial capacity for love—the volume of her devotion to Raymond—was so great that, even after she'd learned for the third time of his faithlessness, something of it remained. But when he showed her that side of him yet again, in moments she found herself utterly emptied.

Robert had had a similar experience with his alcoholic wife. "At the end, Molly's drinking wasn't any different. Actually, I thought I had gotten used to the slovenly house, her mood swings, the crazy accusations, the restaurant scenes. I had always hated the *drinking*, but somehow I had kept on loving *her*. Then last month, she drove our car into the garage—without bothering to open the garage door—and it was over. Eighteen years of marriage. . . ."

In truth, Robert cared little about the garage or the car, both of which Molly had been battering for years. Throughout her many previous incidents, he had been aware only of his *feelings of love* for his wife, despite his despair over her drinking, despair he was able to isolate from the positive feelings the two shared. But gradually, invisibly, Robert's reservoir of love had fallen dangerously low, Molly's brief periods of sobriety providing too little time for replenishment. Her last fender-bender drained away the final few drops.

Obviously, then, any seemingly abrupt end to love

is, in fact, seldom truly sudden. Love is a shield that enables us to endure, with what seems like only transient hurt, the transgressions, inadequacies, and insensitivities of those we care for. But these hurts are not without lasting effect. Love is blind only to the extent that it conceals the degree of injury done until a crucial threshold is reached. Thereafter, there is no going back, no matter the apologies, tears, and promises of the one who has lost his or her partner, no matter the inherent forgiveness of the partner no longer in love. Once lost, romantic love is gone forever. The one-time lovers might go through the motions for a while, but the feelings will have vanished. One never loves the same person the same way twice.

Often, no singular event marks love's demise. Perhaps the relationship was simply a transitional one, part of the growing-up process, and had run its course.

"I don't really *need* the s.o.b.—I'm *not* dependent on him," Sally insisted for months. "I can walk out on this relationship any time I want. I know that for a fact. I've broken up with Roger half a dozen times."

But at last, after much grief, many sleepless nights, and a case of Chardonnay, Sally was able finally to let go, once and for all, of this extraordinarily addicting and destructive relationship. He had been the most exciting—and, incidentally, the most violent and irresponsible—man she had ever met. It had been a long course of instruction, but at last she had won her degree. For several months thereafter, rather shellshocked, she did not date. She sat at home with her cat and her knitting and discovered soufflés and "Masterpiece Theatre." Then, at a New Year's Eve party given by her closest friend, she met Peter.

Peter, himself still bruised from a recent divorce, was everything Roger was not. "Peter was gentle, empathetic, considerate, loving, and utterly ethical. He kissed the pain away. I started singing again in the mornings. Unfortunately, I also gained a lot of weight—on top of everything else, Peter was a hell of a cook. I guess the way to a woman's heart . . .''

Sally's friends were delighted as well. "He's just what you need." And they were right. All the more reason for consternation when, after a year of contentment, Sally fell out of love.

"I still care for Peter, of course, and tried, unsuccessfully, not to hurt him. I'm afraid there are all kinds of ways to tell someone you care for and respect that you don't love him anymore, but no good ways. But the passion, the excitement, they got lost, somehow. It sounds terrible, I know, but suddenly, Peter became . . . irrelevant.''

Peter had been the ideal man to help Sally heal after the addictive catastrophe of Roger. Now that a cure was effected, however, Peter had ceased to be central to her emotional life. He had done his work—helping Sally clear out the wreckage from her previous romance. Now there was space for new arrivals and new beginnings. Probably, her coming relationships will be great improvements over her earlier ones.

Obviously, all people change with time. Even those who seem much the same outwardly over the years may undergo revolutionary shifts within their psyches and thus, inevitably, in their most intimate connections. Indeed, romantic relationships themselves are among life's strongest catalysts for change. (In my practice, I have seen people change much faster because they were in love than because they were in psychotherapy. Which kind of change is the more cost-effective remains an open question.)

A client of mine described this evolutionary process well: "When I first started dating," she explained, "I must admit I gravitated toward guys who abused me—

not necessarily physically, but enough for me to feel pretty lousy. To tell the truth, as a teenager, I didn't have very much in the way of self-esteem, and I guess I chose guys who confirmed the low estimation I had of myself.''

"Eventually, I got smarter. Harry was the first big change. Never a harsh word from Harry. Mostly he ignored me. But for me, that was a step up.''

"After Harry there was Michael, who kept telling me how beautiful I was, how bright. I didn't really believe it at the time, but I guess I must have taken some of it in because two months after Michael and I broke up, I married Sam, who treats me like a princess. Ten years ago, if a guy treated me like a princess, I would think he was putting me on. Now, I guess I kind of believe I deserve it.''

An earlier section noted that many first marriages are primarily structure-building relationships, most of which follow a well-defined course. Some fortunate couples will share a love experience that envelops both of them for a lifetime and permits them to change and evolve along parallel paths as they go about their busy marital tasks. Time only deepens their connection. But for many others, a crisis occurs when one partner develops in some significant fashion outside of the relationship—perhaps in his or her career. At this point, the relationship either changes or comes apart. A relationship might also simply "wind down" when the partner's growing up is completed or when the children move into peer relationships.

Structure-building relationships reach their terminus in a variety of ways. The couple may abruptly split up, just drift apart, or stay together after a fashion while living entirely separate lives. Divorce, of course, is the more common final path and tends to be drawn out because the partners are giving up so much—so many bonds, so much kinship. Indeed, by now, they are more family to each other than they are to their family of origin. Because of these connections, they have a good chance of becoming friends again after they are no longer husband and wife. As a client of mine remarked, after the dust had settled following the end of a seventeen-year marriage; "I can't say a bad thing about Charles. He was a perfect first husband."

Clearly, if love can end even in those "good relationships" where people have bonded for the "right reasons," it is no surprise that *dysfunctional romance* such as in validation, fusion, and avoidance relationships must inevitably fail. These frequently end in hurtful and destructive fashion, replete with betrayals, as soon as "someone better" comes along. Still, in one sense, we rarely ever fall in love with "the wrong person." Rather, that person is in fact probably "right" for us at that *moment* in our developmental scheme of things. The relationship is not as "bad" as much as it is limited or is, perhaps, a painful, yet a deliberate and necessary lesson.

Love's End Lies in Its Beginnings

The end of a romantic relationship is as much a part of its organic process as its beginning, and as such is already present in seminal form at the outset. Just as death is an integral part of life, since we all start to die the day we are born, so the seeds of a relationship's ultimate dissolution are present and subtly apparent from the first.

Indeed, the basis for a relationship's beginning may constitute the very lethal microbe that eventually kills it. People who marry for money will usually divorce for the same reason. A woman attracted to disciplined men for the stability provided by structure may leave the relationship because it has begun to feel rigid and stultifying. The exciting, go-getting career woman now seems "aggressive," "insensitive" to anything but the demands of her work. The strong, taciturn, masterful man appears ever more closed and controlling. In short, love may disintegrate less because its process has *changed* than because it has *intensified*. What was once subtly compelling has become oppressive. Partners in intimacy sign an unconscious contract and tend to follow it to the end.

Rita grew up needing constant assurance that she was a desirable, worthwhile person. "I guess I never felt appreciated as a kid. My parents never took me seriously. But I could make myself look really pretty, and when I flirted with my father, he noticed."

It didn't take Rita long to learn how to get what she needed from other men as well. Then one day she stumbled upon Tim, a man reared by judgmental, punitive, selfish parents who had, at least, shown him what *not* to be like. Tim resolved always to be loving, generous, supportive, and tolerant of all those he cared about.

As one might guess, Rita and Tim immediately fell in love. But their relationship changed rapidly. Tim initially indulged, then just accepted, and finally barely endured Rita's increasing narcissism, selfishness and flirtatiousness. In time, Rita's behavior became so outrageous that she exceeded even Tim's boundaries. In other words, Rita gratified her abiding need for masculine approval by obtaining it wherever she could, eventually going beyond her lover's enormous neurotic capacity for tolerance and beyond her own ability to pull herself back to him. Paradoxically, the very same enmeshing, symmetrical needs that initially pulled them together now broke their connection.

Danger Signals

As described earlier, love, once established, can withstand a variable but ultimately finite number of insults before it dies. At its wake, the partners may recall incidents contributing to the demise, but unfortunately most people do not become aware that their relationship is in trouble until they have come close to its tolerance threshold. Having used denial, rationalization, or other defense mechanisms to brush away previous misadventures, they are usually in extremis before they decide to seek help.

As a therapist, again and again I see people who are close to terminating a relationship but who try "hanging on" while their partners enter therapy and "shape up." Often it's too late. The relationship has already slipped into bankruptcy. There have been too many "mistakes," too many injuries, too many times that the offending partner failed to take responsibility. At the end, despite treatment, there are one or two more incidents, perhaps trivial ones, and the reservoir runs dry. The relationship is over. Neither saw it coming early enough.

In my experience, love is dying and probably beyond resuscitation when:

- respect and trust are largely gone

- one or both partners must compromise endlessly to sustain the connection

- one or both partners repeatedly assume negative intent on the part of the other, i.e. "You did that to *deliberately* hurt me"

- the needs of one vastly exceed the ability of the other to meet them

- there is increasing distance and silence

- one partner can no longer hear the other

- partners are no longer able to complete even simple transactions, such as choosing a mutually acceptable movie or getting to a dinner-party on time

- partners are living in the past—the principal bond between them is their shared history (much like what one sees at high school reunions)

- there is compelling interest in extramarital relationships

- there is physical abuse.

The end of any loving relationship is painful, and a marital dissolution, particularly so. But even here, although frequently we counselors fail in our efforts to help a sickly marriage thrive again, we can often assist the former partners to make a success of their divorce. Even love whose last moments are exquisitely hurtful and difficult can be said to end successfully if it makes possible a better new beginning.

VIII

Remedies

The best antidote writers, therapists, or teachers have for any grandiose delusion that we've covered a subject clearly and comprehensively is to take a few questions. In this next section, I offer some representative transcripts from question and answer sessions I've held, and which address the most frequent difficulties encountered in the course of romantic relationships.

1. The Evolution of One's Own Romantic Pattern

Q. *For me, your descriptions of the various patterns of love were entirely too true to life. I'm afraid I find myself, or at least a part of myself, in almost every example. Psychologically speaking, is it possible to be in more than one place at one time?*

A. Yes. For the sake of clarity, I've chosen relatively pure examples to help delineate each configuration. Many people, however, particularly those moving from one major phase of their lives to another, may be captured by a relationship that embodies several patterns, reflecting both where they're coming from and where they are going. And of course, it is not unusual to utilize several psychological processes while establishing a loving connection, some more workable, more useful, than others.

Most people go through a number of romantic relationships while on their way to what I have called the "synergistic" or "mature" connection. I'm sure many of you have had the experience of spending perhaps an evening or so, after long absence, with someone with whom, five years before, you had been head over heels in love, only now to find yourself wondering. "What was *that* all about?" What it was about was this evolutionary process—five years ago you needed to be with him or her in *that* way. You then grew through it making possible the more highly evolved relationships that followed.

For example, you might start off with experimenting, then settle into a structure-building marriage, leave that and enter into a brief healing relationship, and from there evolve into a mature or synergistic connection. Complicating this picture is the possibility that you and your lover have met at a common fork in the road and are traveling together for a relatively few miles before again moving off in different directions and into different kinds of relationships. Thus, the eight pattern types I have presented are really only single snapshots of what is, in fact, a moving process in a continuous state of flux. It's hard to get a good photograph of a shooting star.

2. Interrupting a Destructive Pattern

Q. Why do I seem to have the same fruitless, frustrating kinds of love relationships again and again, and am I doomed to them for the rest of my life?

A. First, if your successive lovers over time seem to be alike, we have to assume that when you were young you were in some way programmed—groomed, if you will—for these particular kinds of relationships. Perhaps there were experiences in your childhood and formative years that made these relationships seem fitting, familiar, ''friendly,'' even compelling, despite your ultimate disappointment or pain. They were as comfortable as an old shoe, and you knew how to participate in them because you were trained in them.

But over the years, you've changed. Your feet have gotten larger, or perhaps you've worn some holes in the soles of your ever tighter shoes. From your question, it appears you are now recognizing these relationships and their limitations—a first step in replacing them with something else. It won't happen all at once though.

People wrestling with your all too common predicament typically hit upon one of two solutions, and you may well discover either of them operating for you:

1. You are somehow arranging each new relationship to be a little better than or at least a little shorter than the previous one. The new partner is less egregious in the kinds of personality traits or conduct that causes you such stress, or you are able to free yourself more quickly from this latest relationship than from its predecessor.

2. The other pattern involves the opposite tack. Here, to set yourself free, you unconsciously fall in love with a partner who exemplifies the *ultimate* in these relationships you find so stressful and frustrating. This experience is then so extreme, so outrageous, that at last, you've had it! You overdose or, as the kids say, get so ''grossed out'' that your

psyche finally says, "never again." At that point, you're ready to move on.

Neither solution is without cost, but either is preferable to staying stuck where you are.

3. Assessing the High Cost of Certain Relationships

Q. I've had four years of psychoanalysis.

A. Congratulations. You must be financially very well off.

Q. I used to be. But I've gotten a great deal from my expenditure. At the very least, I've learned a lot about myself, how I got to be who I am and why I do the things I do. I've gained considerable intellectual insight into how I repeatedly set myself up with relationships that ultimately prove destructive. Each time, I can look back and see just what I've done. But when I'm starting a relationship, and even while I'm in the middle of it (before things get lousy) it feels terrific. It feels like this time it's going to be different. I just don't see the garbage coming until it hits me. It's like I understand the pattern but not the particulars. Is there some way I can go about this differently so that I don't spend the rest of my life bouncing in and out of relationships that start off wonderfully but always seem to leave me with ashes in my mouth? What am I doing wrong?

A. First, you may have the psychological version of a syndrome pervasive in our society—creditcarditis. Second, I suspect you're very good at not looking at price tags.

Having a credit card enables you to grab right then and there, something you think you really want, "paying" for it by laying down a piece of plastic. Since you don't have to reach into your wallet and count out the bills, you don't even have to look very closely at the price tag to see whether or not you've got that much money. By not having to pay for something until tomorrow, people can indulge the feeling that they've obtained it without the pain of paying for it.

Of course, it's human nature to be selectively inattentive to price tags, and indeed, every merchant knows how to exploit this all too common trait. For example, if you've got your heart set on that spectacular BMW, you probably don't go into the showroom to price it but to savor its virtues; and to make sure that this is precisely what occurs, the salesman encourages you to go for a test drive, feel the cashmere upholstery, peek at the V-8 atomic pile under the hood . . . should you bring up price, he'll quickly switch to a discussion of its high resale value or perhaps its indomitable European suspension.

Admittedly, if you shop at Mervyns or Sears, the price hits you in the face (although even there it'll say $49.99 rather than $50.00). But shop at a flashy boutique, and you'd be hard pressed to even *find* a price tag, and should a price be given, it is likely coded or buried in other data. What I'm suggesting is that, when you are caught up in the passion of what you want, it's very easy not to give consideration to what you may have to pay for it. I suspect something of this sort happens whenever you meet someone who really turns you on.

The trick for you, then, is to stop every step of the way and say, "Hmm, this feels good. *How much is it?*'' Every time someone feels really terrific, stop, turn 'em over, and check for the price. You'll find it if you just take a few moments to look. You may still decide to go forward, figuring, "What the heck. It's worth it."; but at least there won't be any surprises this time. You'll know exactly what's coming. And you'll be in a position to cut your losses if, with this added insight, you see that the price is just too high.

Returning to my BMW example: Suppose you feel you've got to have it. You're enchanted by its tight cornering or luxurious interior. So you tell yourself that forty thousand dollars spread out over six years isn't that much. But six years of a miserable relationship is a very long time. It would be better, then, that every time the salesman points out one of the car's spectacular features, you ask him the total sale price. He'll say "Forty thousand, but it has eight super-charged cylinders." You must say, "Tell me again, *how much* will it cost me for those eight super-charged cylinders?" He'll say, "Forty thousand, but it has a splendiferous gold-plated driveshaft." And you ask, "Yes, but how much will that splendiferous gold-plated driveshaft cost me?"

The trick is to connect repeatedly what you *now* want with what you must *later* pay. You might still decide it's worth it, but at least the decision will be a conscious one. You will not be using some mental sleight of hand to suppress awareness of the true cost to you.

For example, a woman applying such counsel to an emerging passion for a married man might say to herself, "God, he's gorgeous; *but, so are his wife and kids*." She never allows herself to imagine him outside the context of that family photograph on his nightstand. Maybe he's so terrific that the relatively modest piece she's likely to get of him is worth the anguish of not having all of him, but she ought to be sure she's decided that worth consciously each time she indulges herself with the available parts.

Pay now rather than later, and you'll pay a lot less. Go out and have a good time in your usual way if that's what you want to do; but remember, in love, as in all things, there is no free lunch. Don't wait until the end of the meal before tallying up the bill. Check the prices, course by course, when you are first handed the menu.

4. Strengthening One's Power to Choose

Q. All the people I've had romantic relationships with have always been more aggressive, more persistent than I am. I find it very hard to take the initiative, to make things happen, so they usually do the choosing. I guess I don't like being forward or pushy or maybe running the risk of rejection . . .

A. I can understand that, but what you are doing is putting *all* power in *their* hands. You have a kind of veto, I suppose, but the lovers who get through to you and rope you in are, as you say, usually the most persistent and aggressive ones. And those qualities may not be the best ones for an enduring relationship. I'm reminded of that epigram about presidential elections—that any man with the aggressiveness and ruthlessness to be a good candidate may not have the best qualities to be a good president. So, although it may be easier to ride the horse in the direction that it is already going, to ensure getting the best possible relationship for yourself, you may not be able to abdicate responsibility for bringing it about. Granted, you can't force a relationship into being, but you can certainly have a say in the process and you certainly can and should declare yourself. Whenever you sense yourself being pressured, stop for a minute and ask yourself: Whose life is this, and what do *I* want to do with it?

5. Connecting with the "Right" Person and Eluding the "Wrong" One

Q. I meet a fair number of very nice women. Now this is gonna sound awful, but . . . they're dull—each and every one. On the other hand, "bad" women— the ones that are kind of flamboyant and wild— they're a trip, but they inevitably screw up my life. I really feel stuck.

A. You're going to stay stuck as long as you unconsciously prize immediate accessibility, ease, and excitement—that quick flush of ready and familiar passion—over true contentment. You haven't come to terms with the "bad" portions of yourself, and I do not use "bad" in a pejorative sense. I'm merely talking about the part of *you* that is a bit thoughtless, perhaps a little reckless, less respectful of your happiness, and now and then willing to participate in screwing up your life. As long as this is a big part of *your* psychic structure, you'll find no shortage of people willing and able to collaborate. Once again, when *you* change, *they'll* change. It sounds like the qualities in a woman that currently attract you are easily visible to you, palpable, even urgent. Other traits, which might lead to an enduring and satisfying relationship, are more subtle and, I gather, for you more difficult to discern. (By the way, these qualities might be immediately apparent to someone with a different make-up who, in turn, would be utterly mystified by *your* choices.) Because you do not perceive the "right" women's most sterling qualities, in their company you instead experience the *absence* of something and feel bored and restless. The companionship of what you call your "bad" women on the other hand, is distracting. They absorb all of your attention and confuse your powers of discrimination. It's tough to hear a string quartet playing a concert just for you, however beautifully, if at the same time you've got a rock band blasting away on your stereo.

Q. *Are you saying I should stop spending time with people I'm naturally attracted to and actively search out opposite types to have a really good love relationship?*

A. No. For one thing, as I indicated earlier, I don't think you can force the process. You can't *make* good relationships happen, however actively you search for the "right" person. But, I do think that when you work to clarify what is really right for and truly fits you, more appropriate people will seek you out. Or rather, you'll find each other. When you change, the signals you send also change. If you switch channels on your psychic CB radio, you will receive messages from some very different kinds of people.

Q. *I'm reminded too much of myself by Elaine—the woman who was always involving herself with boozers. Well, all the men I meet seem to be heavy drinkers or druggies. Is this likely a result of poor judgment on my part—that I go about meeting new men in the wrong way in the wrong places? Or do you think it reflects some deeper psychological problem? Suppose I were never to set foot again in a bar?*

A. That'll help. But implicitly you have raised the question: "Why am I spending so many of my evenings in bars?" Obviously, if there's where you tend to meet your men, you're raising the odds of falling in love with a drunk. But not everyone who goes to bars are heavy drinkers, and there are drunks who prefer to drink at home. My experience leads me to suspect that if you met all your beaux at Christian Fellowship picnics, and if at these picnics there were one or two men predisposed to substance abuse, you would quickly find each other. Lovers or potential lovers sharing a certain process send out some sort of beacon by which they home in on each other. So, staying out of bars is probably a good first step, but you will still have to examine how a predilection to addiction fits into your psychic life.

6. Homosexual Couples

Q. *Do the dynamics and patterns you describe apply to homosexual couples as well?*

A. I think so. I don't really have a large enough database—maybe half a dozen couples at most—on which to draw solid conclusions, but their processes seem entirely the same, though resonant with other overtones.

7. Reading One's Sexual Signal

Q. I am really puzzled by the frequency with which I'm attracted to someone and think it would really be nice to have sex with them, and then, afterward, I discover I'm really not attracted to them in that way at all. It doesn't happen all the time, but often enough to make me wonder.

A. Many people are surprised to discover that even very attractive, personable individuals to whom they are drawn in some way are not, in fact, people with whom they enjoy intimacy. Despite their surface looks, the myriad connections that make for a lively melding just aren't there. On the other hand, these connections may be abundant in someone you do not find classically handsome or beautiful (a good thing, since most of us wouldn't do very well in Hollywood). Perhaps that's one of the principal functions of *experimental* relationships—to enable you to make these kinds of distinctions and more accurately to interpret your own sexual cues.

You are also raising the issue of what I call automatic sex: Just as there are those who routinely salt their soup before tasting it, there are people who "go to bed because he/she was there." Even putting aside questions of morality and health, automatic sex is seldom great sex, however technically proficient the partners.

8. Heightening Passion

Q. We've been married eight years now. We've both been married before, each raised two kids, and now have a marriage that pretty much fits what you call the synergistic, mature relationship. I think so, anyway. We're very loving toward each other, enjoy many of the same things, really enjoy each other's company more than anybody else's. But I'm a little worried because that sexual passion, which you say often helps intensify a relationship, has sort of faded away. Some of it's still there, some of the time. But it used to be a lot better. Fifty-three is too young to be over the hill, isn't it?

A. Sure it is. In my suggestions, I'm going to put aside questions of technique itself since, if the two of you had exciting sex at one point in your relationship, I have to assume that technique is not the problem. Besides, there are plenty of good books available on technique written by some very competent sexual mechanics. So let me respond by focusing on sex within the larger context of your relationship as a whole.

To begin with, you may be taking sex somewhat for granted. Early in a relationship, when you have the benefit of novelty and those first flushes of passion, your sexual appetite alone can overcome such inattentiveness. But familiarity breeds fatigue, and so, later on, irrespective of how much you love each other, the sexual part of your connection may need a sharper focus.

I find many people often so inattentive to matters of sexuality that they hardly have a sense of what their own sexuality is *really* like, no less their partner's preferences. Lovers need to explicitly consider and tell their partners about their erogenous zones. People who take responsibility for their sex lives have better ones than those who trust to mother nature. Granted, you can readily obtain all the vitamin C you need by eating three pounds of turnips a day, if turnips happen to be lying around, but you may be much happier seeking out and getting it from a single kumquat.

Those who tell their lovers precisely what they want and yet still do not receive it may have to work on a possible psychic hearing loss in their partners, or perhaps on some idiosyncrasy in their way of asking. I recall one woman I had in therapy who reported wordlessly squeezing her boyfriend's buttocks tightly against her in an effort to modulate his overzealous thrusting. Unfortunately, he thought she was pressing him on, so he would try ever harder.

People who typically fail to get what they want sexually because they don't request it should ask themselves: Do I know how to put what I want into words? Is it unseemly to reveal that I enjoy certain acts to the point where I ask for them? Do I feel undeserving? Greedy? Wanton? Do I expect to be rejected or disappointed in the event that I do ask?

With practice, one should be able to develop a short series of simple, declarative sentences with which one is comfortable and that fit one's feelings: "Squeeze me there rather than tickle." "When you rub me there, less is more."

If specific directions feel controlling, mechanical, or simply unromantic, more general positive comments may do almost as well: "That's real nice . . . that's wonderful . . . that's even better . . . right there like that—want *lots* of that." Finally, if all words fail, an increment in sighs, moans, and encouraging movements can be used as nonverbal reinforcers of your partner's lucky shots.

Many people simply do not allow time for the shift from worldly concerns or self-preoccupations to intimate nonsexual togetherness and then on to sexual connectedness. Or, even if they move easily to erotic feelings, they may not allow for the buildup of high levels of arousal before going on to sexual release. Such elevations are usually most reliably reached during sexual contact that is coupled with restraint: gratification delayed is gratification intensified. That is, the longer release is deferred, the more erotic the experience becomes. You may remember adolescent petting experiences—the excitement in these events obviously is not testimony to better technique but to the virtues of *not* having what you want when you think you want it.

In this day of ubiquitous fast food parlors, if you are hungry but in a hurry you can "successfully" bolt down a hamburger and a cup of coffee in less than five minutes and feel sated. Compare that, however, to the satisfaction derived from a seven-course banquet spread out over several hours and set in a pleasing ambience. Anyone who proclaims a protracted sexual feast impractical must forego at least some complaints about the lack of sexual satisfaction.

There's one more little problem that sometimes gets in the way of good sex and is easy to solve: Most people have sex at night when they are assured of a block of time together, when work or the children are out of the way, and so on. But the inevitable distracting events of that day, fatigue, alcohol, a heavy meal, and so on can all have a marked anti-libidinal effect. I often suggest that patients meet "for lunch" or, if they simply cannot connect until evening, that they skip dinner in favor of an early bedtime. If still hungry afterwards, they can always send out for pizza.

Incidentally, as men age, there is a change in the time of day when their sexual biorhythm and con-

sequent peak potency occurs—typically to earlier in
the day. One patient who reported he could "barely
get an erection once the sun went down" proved
insatiable at noon.

9. Exploring One's Sexual Self Versus Dying From AIDS

*Q. I hate to bring this up, but, at age twenty-three,
I'm just starting to find out what kind of woman I
am and what kind of man might fit best for me—
just as an AIDS epidemic is starting to roll. Sex is
hardly the only thing I need to check out with a
man, but certainly it is important—at least to me.
How I feel physically about someone tells me a lot.
But I don't want to die while learning. Today I
read that even condoms aren't one hundred percent
safe, and they're such a drag anyway. Any suggestions, or do I just wait for the vaccine?*

A. My answer's a radical one, but absolutely sound,
both physiologically and psychologically: For the
most part, *you do not risk AIDS by having sex.*
That is, touching, kissing, tuning into each other's
sexual rhythms, wrapping around each other, sharing each other's most intimate secrets, achieving
climax external to a bodily orifice—none of this
transmits AIDS. What can give you AIDS during
sexual contact is a presumed carrier achieving penetration. (For men, the reciprocal holds: The like-
lihood of contracting AIDS is nil in the absence of
penetration.) Although these relatively few coital
moments will never be unpopular (and obviously
are the primary reason God or nature created sexuality in the first place), from my perspective, they
are least important to those aspects of sex addressed

in your question: finding out about yourself and, particularly, yourself in relationship to "him."

Ninety percent of sex takes place between your ears, and there's your *entire* body and his *entire* body to consider. Now no one this side of a frontal lobotomy is going to find something good to say about AIDS, but it does at least require that people pay less attention to genitalia and more to *whose* genitalia it is. In other words, a new and virologically unproven lover should not be permitted to come inside you, but he can still come to know your insides and you, his.

10. Finding Someone Truly Worthy

Q. I don't think I'm being arrogant when I tell you that I'm a smart, competent person, and rumor has it that I'm more than a little attractive. Certainly I don't lack attention from members of the opposite sex. I went steady for almost four years while in high school and lived with a man during my last two years of college. When he graduated, he went off to the Marines, of all places. I finished college, and our relationship sort of faded away. Since that time—nothing. I'm twenty-seven-years old and haven't had a decent relationship in five years. I've rarely found a reason to continue seeing most of the men with whom I've gone out past the first or second date. Either they're not very bright, or they're not bright in the same way I am—I always seem to have to explain myself; or they're insensitive, or have no sense of humor, or don't brush their teeth, or something. I do not think I'm weird or especially picky, yet I see plenty of women who seem genuinely contented with men who have less on the ball than your three pounds of turnips. It's bad enough that there are only thirteen years between ages twenty-seven and forty. I certainly don't want to spend them alone. But that's the way things seem to be headed. Can you cheer me up a bit?

A. A bit. You may be a victim of "the pyramid problem."

There are maybe fifteen pyramids in the whole world: a half a dozen or so in Egypt, a bunch in the Yucatan, a couple in Sri Lanka. That's about it. Now if you were one of the lower stones on any of those pyramids, say fifty feet off the ground, or even somewhere in the middle, say one hundred or so down from the top, you would have thousands, maybe hundreds of thousands of compatible stones at or very near your level, all within reach in your home pyramid. There would be almost as many stones above you from which to choose (if you're ambitious), and hundreds of stones to pick from beneath (if you wanted to slum a bit). You could have a reasonable egalitarian date with a different stone from your own neighborhood every night.

But let's say that you have so much going for you that you're placed at the very tip of the pyramid. Inevitably, the higher one goes, the fewer the stones, and the stiffer the competition. At the top, you're practically alone way up there, and there are precious few stones in the rows just below you. The nearest stone at *your* rarified level is all the way over on the next pyramid, a mile or perhaps even a continent away.

In other words, now that you have matured and are perhaps approaching full development, there may indeed be relatively few people worthy of a deep emotional attachment for you. Certainly, there will be no shortage of men looking up at you, hoping to take you out, and you need never lack for companionship. But if you're looking for a serious and enduring relationship with somebody *at* or even a bit *above* your level, it's a long time between drinks or, should I say, between stones.

In our teens, we are pretty much alike. We are captured by similar music, dress uniformly, and share many of the same easy prejudices. By our twenties, we start clumping into disparate but still large, heterogeneous groups. In our thirties, however, the groups become smaller and are distinctly different from each other. By our forties, now fully differentiated and in touch with our own uniqueness, in many ways we may stand almost alone. This process is most rapid and complete in people with the most to work with—those who have the depth, complexity, and artistry to permit so total an individuation.

But remember, there *are* other pyramids out there, and they all have stones at the top facing your very same dilemma. Sooner or later, you'll spot each other; although it's lonely at the top, you do have to accustom yourself to the paradox that the better you are, the longer it takes.

Please understand that we're talking about finding a thoroughly *worthy*—not a *perfect*—person. That *perfect* person is too busy waiting for another *perfect* person to waste time with mere mortals like you and me.

11. Unrequited Love

Q. I have no problem finding women worthy of love. My problem is that I've fallen in love three times in the past three years, but they never feel the same way about me. Besides being a rather unhappy experience, doesn't that also fly in the face of your "reciprocity" theories?

A. My answer to your question contains some good news and some bad news. Which do you want first?

Q. *I'm no wimp—I'll take the bad news first.*

A. The *bad news* lies in the possibility that you have an unconscious inclination to be attracted to certain women precisely *because* they do not respond. You would hardly be alone in this predisposition, and there are different reasons why a surprisingly large number of people have elements of it. For one thing, it's safe—a sure way of never having to worry about commitment. Perhaps also it confirms suspicions or fears that you are undeserving. (The reciprocal would be that the women who have connected with you have a corresponding need to reject any man who might genuinely care for them.)

    The *good news* is that once you can get a handle on the underlying low self-esteem or discomfort with intimacy, the problem with unrequited love often disappears.

Q. *That may take me a while. What do I do in the meantime?*

A. I have some more good news for you. Your feelings of love are likely to have a powerful effect upon the woman inspiring them. With few exceptions, your willingness to open your heart is bound to touch her inside. Without doubt, love itself can be a powerful attractant. Adoration seduces.

    If, however, you begin to express your intense

feelings well before she's ready to receive them—
either from you or from anybody else—they can
have the opposite effect. Unprepared for the
changes within her that your devotion might generate, she may, in fact, back away.

So, although I know this can be difficult, try to
delay or modulate verbal or behavioral expressions
of *your* strong romantic emotions to allow for the
evolution of *hers*. Eventually, you may well find
her far more favorably inclined than if you sent her
a dozen roses every night. Admittedly, if that
essential, underlying psychological fit is lacking,
there's probably little you can do to *make* things
happen. But it is entirely possible that you know
something she doesn't, or you know it a lot sooner.
Often, you just have to give people a bit more time
to discern what you recognize almost at once. So
be patient. It may take a month or a year, but if
something real is hidden there, most likely, you'll
get your chance.

12. Passion That Endures

*Q. My wife and I have been married for forty-seven
years, and I must say, there's still considerable
passion in our relationship. Rearing our three children, if anything, brought us closer together. Incidentally, it was the first marriage for each of us.
Are we exceptions to what you said about the
structure-building relationship?*

A. Yes and no. I have no doubts that the two of you
did some structure-building during the course of
your relationship. But if you are happily and pas-
sionately married after almost five decades, then
there is a much stronger basis for your relationship

than bricks and mortar. If, as I suspect, you have an emotionally solid relationship that evolves as each of you as individuals do, then the arrival of children can act as an intensifier. Without that synergistic and mature emotional connection, however, the rearing of children or the stress and strain of building or redecorating that big new house can act as a detriment to your primary romantic bond. I can't tell you how many people, seemingly contented for ten or twelve years, are finally able to afford that big home and, within a year of moving into it, get a divorce. Why? Their relationship was already running on reserve, and that new house just drained all the remaining energy, leaving them on empty.

But if you have a truly functional emotional partnership, such as the two of you enjoy, then the house, the children, or whatever provide even more for the two of you to share—generating additional strands to your already thriving connection.

Q. *I have the opposite problem. I've been married and divorced twice. Last year I met a man I've come to care for deeply, and we are planning to marry . . .*

A. The triumph of hope over experience?

Q. *I suspect so.* He's *been married and divorced* three *times. My question is: Are we kidding ourselves? Doesn't this bespeak a pattern of marital or relationship failure that's likely to be continued this time as well?*

A. To give you a clinical opinion worth anything, I would need more data about your previous relationships, his previous relationships, why they all ended, and what changes the two of you have made in the interim. I can say this, however:

Consciously and unconsciously, we do learn from experience. It would surprise me greatly if this new relationship the two of you presently enjoy was not in many ways head and shoulders above that of your first marriages and significantly above your subsequent marital relationships.

Whether advanced enough to give both of you what you now want, or even whether or not both of you really want one permanent relationship, I cannot tell. But I have seen many, many people with seemingly dismal track records who in their forties go on to form an inordinately gratifying marital union that lasts for the rest of their lives.

13. Love Everlasting

Q. I've got this sense from you that romantic love is really quite fragile. Is there anything we can do to strengthen it so that it does last forever, or are most such relationships doomed to sort of run their course and come to an end?

A. Of course love need not end. There will always be glowing love affairs that encompass the remainder of the lovers' entire lives. These splendid relationships can go on forever.

All romantic relationships have an ebb and flow. Those likely to endure are the ones where replenishment equals or exceeds what slips away. This replenishment may not always be possible, but there are several effective things most of us can do to enhance the process:

1. Remember that even though a crisis and its

pain seems to be past, things really don't "blow over." The hurts, though forgotten, are not without cost. Go back and talk it over. Try to understand what and how injury was done. Take every opportunity to replace what might have been lost.

2. Explicitly make time for intimacy. Nature has made inexhaustible provision for passion (I have seen couples in their eighties who are sexually active), but one must provide the setting wherein such passion can take place. Save perhaps for the first few months of courtship, sexual union is statistically a rare occurrence during the vacuuming of a rug.

3. Try to recognize and attend to those initially compelling traits that possess a destructive potential. Attempt to identify and cast out, or at least reduce, those characteristics now so addictive, counterproductive, and potentially lethal.

4. Should you encounter a serious problem that the two of you, with all the goodwill in the world, seem unable to overcome, it is not failure to seek professional help—unless one goes too late. Then, it may indeed be a "*last*" resort. A good relationship is not one free of problems, but one that has developed a means to solve them. Six counseling sessions early in a crisis are worth more than six months of psychotherapy at the end.

5. Above all, remember that it is neither cynical nor glib to describe love, like much in nature, as having its season. Almost all the loveliest living things regularly leave us for a time and, with equal reliability, return.

Are you feeling OK about yourself?
Or still playing destructive games?
THE 15-MILLION-COPY
NATIONAL BESTSELLER BY
Thomas A. Harris, M.D.

I'M OK—
YOU'RE OK

00772-X/$4.95 US/$6.50 Can

**The Transactional Analysis Breakthrough that's
Changing the Consciousness and Behavior of People
Who Never Felt OK about Themselves.**

In *I'M OK—YOU'RE OK* find the freedom to change,
to liberate your adult effectiveness and to achieve a
joyful intimacy with the people in your life!

*And continue with a practical program for lifelong
well-being with*

STAYING OK
70130-8/$4.95 US/$5.95 Can

by Amy Bjork Harris
and Thomas A. Harris, M.D.

on how to maximize good feelings, minimize bad ones,
and live life to the fullest!

THE NATIONWIDE
#1
BESTSELLER

the
Relaxation
Response

by Herbert Benson, M.D.
with Miriam Z. Klipper

A SIMPLE MEDITATIVE TECHNIQUE
THAT HAS HELPED MILLIONS
TO COPE WITH
FATIGUE, ANXIETY AND STRESS

Available Now—
00676-6/$4.95 US/$5.95 Can

from the author of

YOUR MAXIMUM MIND
70664-4/$4.50 US/$5.50 Can